ly the Nunnery Quadrangle, ano...
...and in the rear, the Governor's...
...the Quadrangle of the Pigeons; a li...
...of Juab, Lope; Nojeat, Itzd...; and the...

Aerial view of Uxmal. On the rig...
the left, the Pyramid of the Magicia...
nor's Palace, the House of the Turtles...
and the Great Pyramid. Photo courtes...

GUIDE TO
PUUC REGION

UXMAL, KABAH, SAYIL, XLAPAC, LABNA

Schooley
May 91

PROFR. GUALBERTO ZAPATA ALONZO

TABLE OF CONTENTS

GUIDE TO PUUC REGION
Profr. Gualberto Zapata Alonzo.

© Profr. Gualberto Zapata Alonzo.
   Calle 63 No. 437 A
   Tel. 23-08-56
   Mérida, Yuc.
© Producción Editorial Dante, S.A.
   Calle 59 No. 472
   Mérida, Yuc. Méx.
   C.P. 97000

Queda hecho el depósito que marca la ley
ISBN 968-7232-38-2

Impreso en México
Printed in Mexico

NOTICE

Because some readers may not have had the opportunity of perusing our descriptive guide to Chichén Itzá, we find we must repeat certain portions contained therein, as they cover basic information on the Maya Culture that the reader must have in order to get a clearer and more precise concept of the historical past of this incredible Maya nation, particularly in relation to its evolutionary periods, the sources of available information, the great intellectual advances it achieved, and so forth.

We also wish to clarify that the word "complete", as used in the heading, is relative, since a really complete guide book would entail a much larger volume, and that is not our objective. The word "complete" is used only in comparison with other published guide books.

I also wish to thank my good friend and excellent professional photographer, José López Nájera, for his kindness in allowing me to publish in this book, his magnificent photographs (especially, the aerial ones), which are otherwise most difficult to obtain.

The Author

INTRODUCTION

At the time of the Spaniard's arrival in the mid 16th Century, the Maya Culture in Yucatán had been essentially dead for 345 years, partly because of a civil war between Mayapán and Chichén Itzá in 1196, which affected various ceremonial centers in the northern part of the peninsula.

With the defeat of Chichén Itzá in this conflict, the majority of its inhabitants emigrated to Guatemala, and settled in Tayasal, along the coast of Lake Petén Itzá.

Those who did not emigrate, spread in many different directions, and those who were captured were subjected to slavery. Mayapán exerted total domination for the next 245 years (from 1196 to 1441).

Those years were marked by noticeable decadence, since at the time Chichén Itzá, Uxmal, Izamal and possibly other important centers, were abandoned and cultural activities ceased in the whole region.

In 1441, almost all the inhabitants of the peninsula rose in rebellion against the injustices, oppressions and onerous taxation imposed by the governors of Mayapán, and after many bloody battles, with victories and defeats for both sides, Mayapán was finally besieged and totally destroyed. All the chieftains were executed, with the exception of two close relatives of the Cocome dynasty of Mayapán, who were on a bartering trip in Ulua, Guatemala.

Tutul Xiu, a descendant of the nobles of Uxmal, who had hoisted the flag of rebellion, suggested to the peninsula's inhabitants that it might be preferable for each district chieftain to stake out his own territory and govern it as he saw fit; thus, the peninsula was divided into 19 districts.

These districts were under the leadership of chieftains with unlimited power and authority, who governed according to their whim and fancy. These supreme authorities held the title of "Halach Uinic", meaning powerful man; they were also called "Ahau" meaning king or lord.

The Mayas of that decadent period lived in straw or palm thatched huts, in small or middle-sized villages, almost like when the nation first began to emerge prior to the Christian era. Their social structure was but a pale reflection of what it had been at the height of their glory.

Upon being abandoned in 1196, the buildings of the archeological centers today known as Uxmal, Kabah, Labná, Chichén Itzá, Izamal, and others of northern Yucatán, were taken over by dense vegetation; tree roots cracked the walls and brought the buildings tumbling down, to be covered again. Eventually, most of them looked like natural hillocks.

Such were the conditions of the peninsula and its inhabitants upon arrival of the conquistadors.

Unfortunately, most of the Spaniards that came to this land at that time were almost illiterate, and instead of researching the glorious history of these ancient inhabitants of Yucatán, they went out of their way to destroy everything that lay in their path. Only very few bothered to collect historical data and reports.

When the foreign invaders found that Yucatán did not have the anticipated gold and silver mines - one of the major reasons for their venture - they tried to leave Yucatán, especially when they heard that Francisco de Pizarro had found great quantities of gold and silver in Peru. Upon receiving word of this, they immediately wanted to emigrate. It was Captain Francisco de Montejo, Jr. (founder of the city of Mérida) who stopped them by instituting harsh laws to prohibit his countrymen from leaving the peninsula, except in specifically justified cases.

However, to compensate them he divided the territory of Yucatán into "encomiendas" or land grants with specified numbers of natives who were put to work, mainly in back-breaking agricultural labor, and who generally, were little more than slaves. These conditions lasted many, many years, even beyond the time of Mexico's independence.

SOURCES OF INFORMATION

The knowledge available on the history of the ancient Mayas comes from many different sources; however, one of the most valuable was bequeathed by the second Bishop of Yucatán, Diego de Landa, in his well-known "Relation of Things in Yucatán". This cleric did not limit himself to describing the customs and activities of the Mayas of the decadent period, but also carefully researched and recorded the most important historical events of these people by talking to the erudite Maya chieftains then living.

One of the most valuable things he left us was a description of the operation of the 365-day civil calendar in effect at the time, and another system for dating called the "Katun Round", which the Mayas used in recording their most important historical events. He copied the calendrical and other glyphs and described their meanings. Thanks to him, researchers have been able to clarify the meanings of various hieroglyphics that survived.

De Landa realized that the natives had unfortunately used some of their ancient writings in their religious ceremonies and these had to be eliminated so that conversion to Christianity could occur more quickly. He issued an auto-da-fé and ordered that their idols and censers, as well as 27 ancient Maya manuscripts, be burned in the atrium of the church in Maní, on June 16, 1562. Thus, the opportunity to learn more about this culture was lost forever.

Other valuable reports were prepared and collected by the cleric Diego López de Cogolludo, Friar Alonso Ponce, and by the "cabildos" or town councils and the "encomenderos" or land-grant holders, such as Don Martín del Palomar, Diego Briceño, Juan Bote, Pedro García and Juan Cuevas de Santillán.

Further information was found in the Maya chronicles of Chilám Balám, written by the Mayas in their language but with Spanish phonetism. It is known that there were 16 of these chronicles. Eight were lost before being completely analyzed. Of the remainder, the three from Maní, Tizimín and Chumayel have been considered the most important. Each chronicle has been given the name of the place where it was found. These chronicles contain interesting historical data -- prophecies, chronology, religion, medicine, astronomy, and divinations. Contemporary events were also recorded in this manner.

These writings have been enormously valuable in providing important historical details; although some portions appear to be in disagreement with archeological findings.

We would like to take this opportunity to honor one of the most outstanding historians of the Maya epoch, the late lawyer and great expert of the Maya language, Juan Francisco Molina Solís. With incredible patience, he wrote an extremely interesting work, published in three volumes and entitled "Historia del Descubrimiento y Conquista de Yucatán" (History of the Discovery and Conquest of Yucatán). He based his data on the already mentioned information sources and other documents relating to Yucatán, obtained in the archives of Seville, Simancas and the Escorial in Spain. He carefully analyzed all these reports, putting them in order with an admirable sense of logic.

When he wrote the first edition of his book in 1896, no excavations and restorations had yet been made at Chichén Itzá, or at any other archeological sites in Yucatán, and very little was known about the Mayas of this region. However, his conclusions and descriptions, especially with reference to times and eras, are mostly in agreement with the results obtained by the archeologists at a much later date, which shows the effectiveness, precision and importance of his work.

Some scientific information was obtained by studying the three important Maya codices that still survive, which were found in Europe. The longest is the Codex Tro-Cortesianus or Madrid Codex; it is 7.15 meters long and has 56 leaves folded like a screen, or 112 pages. All the codices are folded in this screen-like manner.

Next in size is the Dresden Codex; it is 3.50 meters long, with 38 leaves or folds, or 76 pages.

The smallest codex was found in Paris, and is called the Peresianus Codex; it measures 1.45 meters in length, with 11 leaves or folds, or 22 pages.

Some of the pages of the Dresden Codex are painted in many colors and are beautifully and artistically drawn.

In these codices, scientists have found information on astronomy, chronology, religious rites, agriculture, hunting, sacrifices, food preparation, ritual drinks, wars, and much more.

The learned United States archaeologist, Sylvanus G. Morley, suggests that the codices are part of a Maya encyclopedia, the remaining volumes of which have been lost.

For their writings, the Mayas prepared a type of paper similar to ours, using the white part of the bark of the Yucatán poplar, finely ground, to which they added gum dissolved in water. The gum was obtained from the resin of the cedar and another tree called "pich" in Maya. The pulp thus obtained was probably pressed through two wooden rollers to produce long sheets of paper which were then given a thin coat of lime to make them white. Once dry, these sheets or leaves were folded like a screen, to make handling and protecting easier. Bishop Landa says that the paper was made from the roots of certain trees.

Other data came from archaeologists, anthropologists and explorers, some of whom were financed by national and foreign institutions; and thanks to their tenacity and perseverance, some of the many mysteries of the incredible culture of the ancient Maya have been unraveled.

At a lecture given by this author at the inauguration of the International Maya Congress, held in Mérida, Yucatán, on October 28, 1983, at which approximately 2,300 representatives from 23 countries (mostly archaeologist and anthropologists) participated, he was asked: Why is nothing known of the history of the Mayas from Guatemala, Honduras and adjacent areas? Why are the names of the founders and the dates unknown of when Tikal, Copán, Uaxactún and others were occupied, when that is not the case in northern Yucatán.

The answer was: At the time of the first downfall of the Maya Culture in those regions, in 925 A.D., the so-called ceremonial centers had already been abandoned and had not been used again. Thus, by the time the Spaniards arrived, there had been a very long period of cultural inactivity, and the Mayas of that decadent period, who lived far from those centers, remembered nothing of the mysterious past of their ancestors. On the other hand, in northern Yucatán, the collapse of 925 A.D. was not felt as strongly. In fact, in that region there had been a resurgence which was, especially at Chichén Itzá, incremented by strong Toltec influences.

CULTURAL PROGRESS OF THE
ANCIENT MAYAS

It has been clearly proven that of the ancient cultures

of the American continent, none was more grandiose than the Maya, since in many aspects, it rivaled other Old World cultures. To date, no writing as difficult and complicated as the Maya's has been found. At present, only some 800 glyphs have been identified in the three aforementioned codices, in the reliefs carved on the stelae (stone slabs of different sizes on which the Maya artistically carved important figures and dates in cycles of 20, 10 and 5 years), and in the carvings on lintels, columns and other parts of their buildings; it is not known how many may have been lost.

However, it is known that quite a few years prior to the Christian era, they accomplished the great feat of discovering the mathematical symbol known as zero, the basis of our modern mathematics. It is due to the zero that computers were invented -- helping modern man solve his many complicated problems.

After discovering the zero, the Mayas used it in their ingenious trinumeral and vigesimal system, using a dot or point to represent the unit, the dash or hyphen for the number five, and the zero as a positional; with this system they could count to infinity (millions, billions, etc.). They also had great knowledge of astronomy. In the Dresden Codex, a table was found which indicated 69 solar eclipses in a period of 33 years. In another table, they recorded the rotation of the planet Venus in its orbit with such precision that today's scientists tell us they had an error factor of only 14 seconds. They also figured out the synodic rotation of this planet with extraordinary accuracy. They knew of

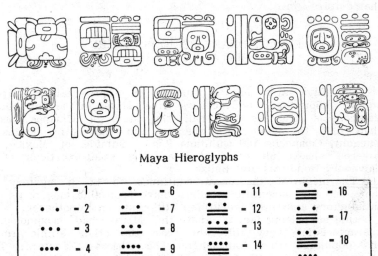

Maya Hieroglyphs

• – 1	•̇ – 6	•̇̇ – 11	•̇̇̇ – 16
• • – 2	•̇ •̇ – 7	•̇̇ •̇ – 12	•̇̇̇ •̇ – 17
• • • – 3	• • • – 8	•̇̇ • • – 13	
• • • • – 4	• • • • – 9	•̇̇ • • • – 14	•̇̇̇ • • • – 18
— – 5	= – 10	= – 15	•̇̇̇ • • • • – 19

Maya numbers 1 to 19 (trinumeral and vigesimal system).

and exactly recorded the lunar cycles, and the seasons of the year.

In the Tro-Cortesianus Codex, a table was found that indicated the signs of the zodiac. In 682 A.D., they developed the most exact calendar known in the world at that time.

For purposes of demonstrating the accuracy of the Maya calendar, we would like to point out its relation to the Julian, Gregorian and scientific calendars: the Julian calendar consists of 365.2500 or 365 and one-fourth days; the Gregorian has 365.2425 days, that is, 75 ten thousandths of a day difference with the Julian. The scientific year has 365.2422 days, or three ten thousandths of a day difference with the Gregorian; and the Maya year has 365.2420 days, differing from the scientific by only two ten thousandths of a day. The incredible thing is that our scientists arrived at this with modern equipment, while the Mayas already had it calculated in 682 A.D. As we all know, in our present system for counting the passage of time, we add one day every four years -- the leap year -- to correct this fraction of almost one-fourth of a day per year.

The Maya architecture is material proof of their great intellectual progress. When we look at their majestic buildings, carried out with such a high sense of esthetics and adorned with such incredible reliefs, executed with precision and elegance, it seems well-nigh an impossible feat, particularly if we remember the era of those constructions and the tools that were used.

This brief description, gives us an idea of how grandiose that culture was.

EVOLUTIONARY PERIODS OF THE MAYA CULTURE

· The Maya area has a surface of approximately 325,000 square kilometers, and covers five states in the Republic of Mexico -- a little less than half the state of Chiapas, more than half the state of Tabasco, and the entire states of Yucatán, Campeche and Quintana Roo. Outside of Mexico, it covered almost all of Guatemala, and small portions of El Salvador, Honduras and Belize.

The origin of the Maya continues to be a mystery -- none of the scientific studies have been able to give us any satisfactory answers, everything still rests on hypotheses.

One surprising fact is that the Mayas had morphological characteristics very different from the other ethnic groups that populated this continent. The Olmecs, Zapotecs, Toltecs, etc., all had features different from the Maya, as can be appreciated in their drawings and sculptures, in idols, murals, ceramics and reliefs. The Maya is more similar to the Japanese or Polynesian, or some race from India. An analysis of this can be found in the book "An Overview of the Maya World", also written by this author.

Some years ago, archeologists calculated that humans had been present in the Maya area since 3000 BC; they had also concluded that those inhabitants first settled in small villages around 800 BC. Subsequent studies, however, placed the date at 1500 BC; then just recently, in 1976, a British expedition exploring a mud and gypsum construction in Belize, found pieces of charcoal that dated from 2500 BC.

Another surprising discovery occurred only a few years ago in the fascinating Loltún cavern, located about 7 kms from the village of Oxkutzcab, and about 110 kms south of the city of Mérida, capital of the state of Yucatán. Loltún

Archaeological map of the Maya Region.

13

is a Maya word meaning stone flower. These caverns are slightly more than 700 meters long, with some branching; in one section of these caverns, there is a chamber called "Huechil". Archaeologists from the National Institute of Anthropology and History (I.N.A.H.) of Mexico, excavating the floor of that chamber, found to their great surprise, part of a mastodon's tusk and molar, the fibula of a bison, the hoof of a small Pleistocene horse and bones from other animals of that same time period.

According to these explorers' reports, those bones were found in association with crudely fashioned lithic tools made of wood and bone, indicating man's presence at the time those animals existed.

Based on stratigraphic studies and on classified ceramics, archeologists have divided the evolutionary periods of the Maya culture in different ways, according to their particular points of view; however, these classifications are not definitive as new discoveries keep changing them.

One of the more generally accepted divisions, as indicated below, is the one put forth by the learned British archeologist, Eric S. Thompson, particularly with reference to the Classic Period, which, according to the most recent discoveries, gives us a general idea of this culture's evolution:

FIRST PERIOD: Pre-Maya - from time immemorial to 2500 BC
SECOND PERIOD: Formative or Pre-Classic - from 2500 BC
      to 200 A.D.
THIRD PERIOD: Classic (subdivided into 3 stages) -
     Early Classic - from 200 to 625 A.D.
     Flourishing - from 625 to 800 A.D.
     Decadent - from 800 to 925 A.D.
FOURTH PERIOD: Mexícan or Toltec - from 925 A.D. to
      1200 A.D.
FIFTH PERIOD: Mexícan absorption (Post-Classic Decadent)
     - from 1200 to 1540 A.D.

Practically nothing is known about the Pre-Maya period, or of the origins of those peoples. During the early stages, they led a nomadic way of life, and towards the end of the period, they began their semi-sedentary lifestyle.

During the Second Period, that is, around 2500 BC, buildings made of perishable materials were first erected, an incipient form of agriculture was initiated, tools of hard stone, wood and bones were fashioned, ceramics appeared, and religious rites and ceremonies came into use. Subsequently, hieroglyphic writing was invented, as well as the numerical system and the calendar; the process for the manufacture of mortar was discovered, by mixing lime with the white earth called "sascab" at a ratio of two or three to one, thus giving rise to architecture. All these discoveries and advances constituted the foundation of the Classic Period.

During the Third Period - the Classic, subdivided into three stages - the Mayas reached the peak of their cultural achievements. They erected their most beautiful buildings, they fashioned their best ceramics and decorated them with masterful drawings, they perfected their calendar, and made their most outstanding astronomical discoveries. But by the year 800 A.D., they began to decline. The ceremonial centers were successively abandoned, starting in the central region and moving northwards to the area known today as Puuc, giving the impression that the Mayas of these regions, disappeared from the cultural scene for reasons still not satisfactorily explained, but most probably because of the rebellion by the laborers against the nobles.

Shortly after this downfall, the Toltecs from Tula arrived in Chichén Itzá, where their strong influence is still very apparent, particularly in architecture, ceramics, paintings, sculptures and religion. It is assumed that it was the Toltecs who introduced the human sacrifices that consisted of opening the chest cavity of the victims, removing the heart, and offering it to their gods during special ceremonies.

At Uxmal, the Toltec influence is not as noticeable; it is observed only in some feathered serpents, in the ball game, in a few ceramic pieces, in a few faces which look like Tlaloc (the Nahua rain god), and some other minor details. This author believes that the Toltecs did not cohabit with the Mayas in Uxmal, as they did at Chichén Itzá, but rather, that these few instances, were simply a cultural reflection that was copied there.

It is quite possible that the arrival of the Toltecs, and their union with the Itzá, produced widespread discontent among the peninsula's inhabitants, and to avoid a civil war, it was agreed, after many discussions between the chieftains of each region, to form a confederation with laws and regulations that would equally protect all the sectors that it represented. So a confederation was born, with the participation of Chichén Itzá, Uxmal, Izamal, Mayapán, and possibly some other important centers. Mayapán was selected as headquarters for this confederation due to its geographic location.

During the period of the confederation, which started in 1002 and ended between 1182 and 1196 A.D., the Maya population lived in peace, solving all problems through diplomacy, this period being noted for its tranquility and success.

Some archeologists and historians deny the existence of this confederation, believing that Uxmal had already been abandoned at that time, but recent explorations carried out at Uxmal by I.N.A.H. archaeologists, have proved that Uxmal's active life continued until the 12th Century, which coincides with the duration of this confederation.

The alliance ended with a civil war between Chichén Itzá and Mayapán. This civil war was won by Mayapán, with the help of Nahua mercenaries who had been brought in from Xicalango, located in the present state of Tabasco.

During the Fifth and last period, 1200 to 1540 A.D., specifically in 1441, almost all the peninsula's inhabitants rose in rebellion; Mayapán was soundly defeated, and the Yucatán Peninsula was divided into 19 districts. And then in 1540, the Spaniards came and conquered.

CHARACTERISTICS OF THE YUCATAN PENINSULA AND LOCATION OF THE PUUC AREA

In the northern part of the Yucatán Peninsula, the soil is extremely rocky, particularly in the coastal regions; dense vegetation, however, inexplicably grows there during the rainy season. Deep soil can be found only in the southern portions of the Peninsula, also the site of its only mountain ranges. The mountains start in the western state of Campeche, then run eastwards into the state of Yucatán; at the city of Ticul, one branch of foothills turns southwards, while another turns westward again, forming a horseshoe, which flattens out and disappears after a few kilometers.

In the northern portion of this Peninsula, there are no rivers or lakes, with the exception of those at Cobá, in the state of Quintana Roo; instead, there are various fresh water sources (some covering almost four acres) that never dry up, but the water is muddy and unfit for human con-

Cenote "Keken" from the village of Dzitnup on east of the Yucatán State.

sumption.

The best water sources, during those ancient times, were the natural wells called cenotes; these cenotes, many of which still exist, vary in shape, dimensions and depths. In places where these natural wells and underground rivers did not exist, the inhabitants solved their water problems by building cisterns, called "chultunes" by the Mayas, in which rain water was collected. Quite a few of these cisterns have been found in places that were inhabited, and it is not known how many thousands may be lost somewhere in the jungle.

In this region, the rainy season starts in mid to late May and ends in September; however, severe storms occur in the Caribbean during the months after that, but these generally head into the Gulf of Mexico. Yucatán receives only intermittent rains and drizzles which, instead of causing property damages, are beneficial to agriculture and live-stock.

Many archeological sites are found along the above-mentioned mountain ranges. In explorations recently carried out in the Peninsula, 1,117 of these sites were identified, but in this book, we shall talk only about Uxmal, Kabáh, Sayil, Xlápak and Labná.

The architecture of this region, has well-defined and ex-clusive features with respect to the ornamentation of the high-relief façades. The stones were cut with such preci-sion and elegance, that it seems impossible that their fine finish was accomplished with tools made of hard stone. This architectural style is known today as Puuc, and it is differ-entiated from other styles by the following details: the relief decorations start at the level of the doors and flow upwards until they cover the entire upper sections of the buildings. In many instances, this decoration consists of small vertical columns embedded in the walls; in others, friezes in associ-ation with diverse motifs are observed; and in still others, grids were made with crosses or exes, which were joined to-gether to give the appearance of latticework. Also common, are stones cut with teeth-like projections which form squares upon being joined; in the center of these, flowers and other motifs were added. In some instances, these dentated, zig-zag stones were alternated with isosceles triangles to dec-orate the cornices. On these same façades, large, stylized masks with long noses like elephant trunks, some trunks curving upwards, others downwards, can frequently be seen. These effigies have been given the name of "Yum Chaac" (the Rain God), but to date, no researcher has satisfactorily explained how it is known that those large masks represent this deity. Each of these masks has a different expression and composition, which suggests to us that if, in reality, they are deities, they do not represent only one.

On the southern side of the so-called Nunnery Quad-

MASKS OF THE SO CALLED "RAIN GOD" SHOWING THE MANY VARIATIONS. Photos by the author.

A) One of the 12 masks on one side of the western stairway of the Pyramid of the Magician.

B) Superimposed masks on the southwest corner of the East Side of the Nunnery Quadrangle.

C) Masks on North Side of this same Quadrangle.

D) Other masks on the North side.

E) Mask located in the central chamber of the Great Pyramid.

F) Two masks on the east corner of the Great Pyramid.

G) Three masks on the west corner of the Great Pyramid.

H) Group of masks located on the upper portion of Kabah's "Codz Poop" Palace.

I) Two superimposed masks on Xlapak's most important building.

J) Mask on the second floor of the Palace at Sayil.

K) Mask on the Palace at Labná.

rangle at Uxmal, there is a stone carving of a straw-thatched hut over each door, and above each hut, there is a large mask; these seem to be the only masks without the trunk-like nose. The noses here are replaced by curvi-linear, cone-shaped triangles with a corn cob in the center.

The present-day Mayas call the afore-mentioned mountain ranges the Puuc. When the archaeologists were looking for a name to describe the architectural style that predominates in this area, they decided to call it Puuc also. The Chenes style is easily differentiated from the Puuc, because its decorations totally cover the façades of the buildings, from floor level to the upper cornice, and in many instances, the doors are carved to represent the enormous mouths of animals or stylized figures.

UXMAL

Because of the number, size and beauty of its buildings, Uxmal is thought to have been the second capital of the Maya people in northern Yucatán during the Classic Period. Uxmal is located 78 kilometers south of the city of Mérida. Today, this archeological center is known for its great architectural beauty. Its name comes from two monosyllabic Maya words: "ux" meaning to bring in (a crop) and "mal" meaning the time or occasion; it could thus be translated as the occasion on which a great crop was brought in. It is speculated that the ancient Maya from the neighboring village of Kabáh (which will be described later and which preceded Uxmal in time), sometimes used this place for planting crops, and on one occasion, obtained an excellent one. Thereafter, when the inhabitants of Kabáh who went there were asked where they were going, they would reply, "to where we brought in the large crop"; in time, this was simplified, and after the area became populated, it continued with that name.

Some of the guidebooks on Uxmal say that originally this place was called "Oxmal", which changes the meaning of the expression, because "ox" in Maya, means three, and "mal" occasion or time. It has been said that this place was occupied and abandoned on three successive occasions. This name and the reasoning are absurd and unacceptable. It is impossible that upon being populated for the first or second time, it would already have the name "Oxmal" or three times. It may be that the Mayas of the Decadent Period called it by that name, after it had been abandoned.

With reference to its history, very little is known as the native chronicles and other historical sources hardly mention it.

As to the date on which Uxmal was founded, there are discrepancies. The dates which the historians used as base, are recorded in the notation system known as the Katun Round or Short Count which is prone to errors when not carefully managed while being correlated with our present calendar.

The report apparently most accepted is provided by the noted historian Molina Solís, as it is the one that most closely matches the archeological explorations. From his descriptions, we gather that during the "fourth Ahau", which dates back to the beginning of the Christian era, a large group of emigrants, under the leadership of Ahmekat Tutul Xiu, headed towards the southern portion of the Peninsula, known at that time as Chacnovitán; that this emigration came from the west, and passed through the

The five-story Palace at Edzná, in the State of Campeche.
Photo by the author.

states of Tabasco and Campeche; that this group progress-
ively founded various settlements along its route, among
which are Xuelén, Zihó, Opichén, Ticul, Kabáh, Sayil,
Labná, Uxmal, etc.; to these, we are adding another two
that are very important, namely, Edzná, in the state of
Campeche, and Oxkintok in the state of Yucatán. At Edzná,
there is a very tall structure of five superimposed floors in
the shape of a pyramid and with houses on top. Oxkintok is
of lesser importance and is located near the village of
Maxcanú in the state of Yucatán (see map of the Peninsula of
Yucatán). These same chronicles indicate that before Mayapán was founded, and while the Itzá were still roaming the
southern jungles, one of Ahmekat Tutul Xiu's descendents,
called Ahcuitok Tutul Xiu, founded Uxmal. This leader
undertook the cultural development of his subjects, teaching
them to cultivate the earth, and teaching the priests all
about the calendar, writing, astronomy, architecture and
other sciences. Those ancient documents say that Ahcuitok
Tutul Xiu was also called Hunikilchac.

From this narrative, we see that Uxmal existed prior to
Chichén Itzá, which was founded in 514 A.D. (or possibly 30
to 60 years earlier).

Another fact about the founding of Uxmal is found in the
report prepared by the cleric, Alonso Ponce, in which he
says that a knowledgeable old, Spanish-speaking Maya from
the village of Maní, was told by his ancestors that Uxmal
had been occupied for more than 900 years; to this we can

add an estimate of the man's age, which we assume was around 60. We also know that Alonso Ponce was in Yucatán in 1588; if we subtract 960 from that, we arrive at the year 628 A.D., as the year in which Uxmal was occupied and populated.

A more accurate date for Uxmal's occupation was provided by Yale University researchers who, just a few years ago, subjected a sapodilla wood lintel from the first substructure of the Temple of the Magician. (west side) to carbon-14 dating, and came up with the year 569 A.D.

Another comparative fact that we could use in trying to solve this enigma is that Oxkintok, believed to be contemporaneous to Uxmal, is the site of the oldest recorded date in the northern part of the Peninsula, and it is equivalent to 475 A.D.

The reader will now be aware of the order of the dates calculated for the founding of Uxmal according to the research mentioned: 464 by the Maya chronicles (50 years prior to Chichén Itzá being occupied); 475 by the Oxkintok lintel; 569 by carbon-14 dating of the lintel; and 628 by Alonso Ponce's report. In terms of history, all these dates are very close to one another. If we also consider, that the building with the lintel in Oxkintok and the first substructure of the Temple of the Magician in Uxmal, were not the first buildings erected, it is possible to calculate the date of Uxmal's founding as occurring during the early 5th Century or possibly even a little before.

Several scientists have insisted that the Itzá of Chichén Itzá, the Xiu of Uxmal, and the Cocom of Mayapán were foreigners. This cannot be accepted for the following reasons: the surnames Itzá, Xiu and Cocom are Maya, and the tribes governed and led by same, all spoke the same language, used the same writing, architecture, religion, etc., with the exception of the changes introduced by the Toltecs at Chichén Itzá during the Post-Classic Period, which started between the years 975 and 987, with the arrival of Kukulcán (the feathered serpent).

Most researchers do not know the origin of the Itzá people, and assume that they were foreigners who arrived in Chichén Itzá at the beginning of the Post-Classic Period. What has confused them is Bishop Landa's description, when he wrote: "It is the opinion of the Indians who populated Chicheniza together with the Yza, that a great master called Cuculcán reigned there, and the principal building called Cuculcán shows this to be true; and it is said he came from the west, and they only differ on whether he came before or after the Yza, or with them." The Indian Chronicles quoted by Molina Solís say that "itzá" is the radical of Itzamná, who was also called Lakin Chan, founder of Chichén Itzá in 514 A.D., which is why the inhabitants there were called either the Chan or the Itzá right from the beginning.

With reference to the name Tutul Xiu, its meaning is authentically Maya, "tu tul" is the gerund of the verb to overflow, "xiu" means forb or grass, and "cocom" is the Maya name of a vine with yellow flowers.

It has been the custom among the Maya, from time immemorial, to use the names of plants and animals and various other expressions as surnames, although the significance of the words are not necessarily related to the person who carries the name.

From the historical data, in association with the archeological data, we might logically deduce that the Mayas arrived in northern Yucatán with their full culture, and although their place of origin is believed to be Nonohual (according to the Chronicles of Chilám Balám), it is possible that it may have been Tikal, Copán, or some other place close by. Logic leads to us to believe that the Mayas referred to in the above descriptions did not come from the west, but from the south, where they had evolved culturally, since their physical features, as well as their art, science, religion, etc., are very different from their Mesoamerican neighbors; and that the first inhabitants of the northern Yucatán Peninsula, whose reminiscences have been found at the various sites, did not evolve culturally.

Our hypothesis is reinforced by the fact that at Edzná, the five structures of its most important building were built on a steeply inclined pyramid built in the Petén style of Guatemala. A wide hole was excavated into the front terrace of the highest structure, allows us to see the beginning of the pyramid's stairway that was covered when the five structures were added.

In addition, Professor Antonio Canto López, in his fascinating book "Apuntaciones sobre Mesoamérica" (Notations on Mesoamerica), says that in Oxkintok, close to Maxcanú and southwest of Mérida, there are some buildings that have glyphs similar to those used in the Petén style, and that the construction of these is remarkably similar to the buildings at Uaxactún, Guatemala. Another fact that supports our hypothesis is that the oldest known structure, E-VII, was found in Uaxactún.

If we look at the archeological map of the Yucatán Peninsula, we note that from Copán, Honduras, to Cobá and Chichén Itzá, there are a number of archeological sites, which run more or less parallel to the Caribbean coast, from where the Chanes or Itzá are said to have originated, according to the Chronicles of Chilám Balám. From Tikal, Guatemala, northwards and into the Puuc region, there appears to be a second chain of sites, some of which are Calakmul, Becan, Pustunich, Hochob, Edzná, Santa Rosa Xlapak or Xtampak, and Keuic. This route may have been the one followed by the Xiu for a number of generations, until they became established at Uxmal, as per these same Chronicles. Therefore, it becomes apparent that the Chanes, or Itza, and the Xiu came from the same ethnic lineage.

DESCRIPTION OF UXMAL

As already noted, it can be unequivocally stated that the architecture at Uxmal was the most beautiful of the American continent during Pre-Hispanic times -- its fine finish, the delicacy of its soft lines, the proportions of its majestic buildings, and the richness of its varied reliefs, are all indications of its builders' high sense of esthetics.

Unfortunately, the original names and the real uses given by the ancient Mayas to their buildings are unknown to us; the reasons for same have already been explained. The Maya culture had disintegrated long before the Spaniard's arrival, and a large number of their masonry buildings were already in ruins and covered by vegetation. Some of the building names used today were given by the first Spaniards that saw them, others were given by the first explorers who came from abroad, and still others were given by the archeologists that restored them.

Almost all researchers believe that all the ancient Maya activities were religious in nature, which is why their towns have been called "ceremonial centers", and their buildings have been designated as temples. For instance, at Chichén Itzá, restorers called one of the most important structures the Temple of the Warriors; the major pyramid was called the Temple of Kukulcán; the annex to the Ball Court, the Temple of the Jaguars; another was named the Temple of the Wall Panels. At Uxmal, the major pyramid was named the Temple of the Magician; a section on the north side of the so-called Nunnery Quadrangle was named the Temple of Venus. An attempt is being made to change the name of the Governor's Palace to the Temple of the Sun, only because recently, some effects of sunlight projections have been observed there at certain times of the year.

The activities of the Maya people must have been very well organized and planned, and they must have had buildings to house their administrative systems; otherwise, without metal tools or draft animals, without the use of the wheel, and, in the Puuc area, without natural wells, they never would have been able to erect the extraordinary buildings which are so majestic and impressive that they continue to astound all who see them, nationals and foreigners alike. We are absolutely certain that the Mayas of those glorious days had palaces in which the nobility lived, and schools in which the nobles' children were educated, since the advanced knowledge that they acquired in writing, mathematics, astronomy, medicine, architecture, economics, etc., had to have been imparted from some appropriate building. Had that not been the case, the cultural downfall would have occurred much sooner. Such educational centers would have been located in the most important cities, and

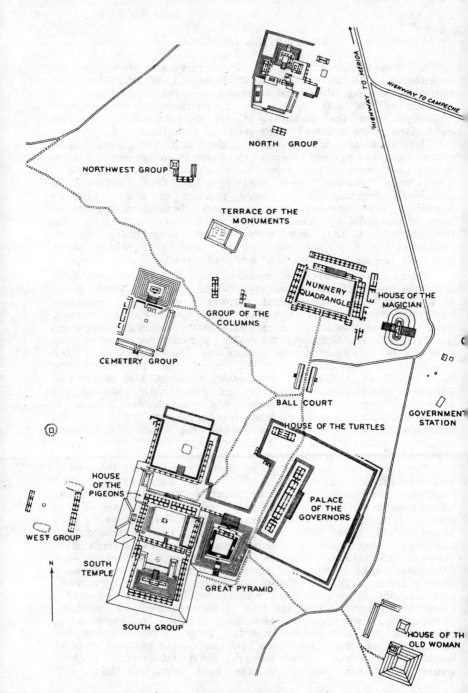

Map of the Central Section of Uxmal
From The Book "The Ancient Mayans" of Sylvanus G. Mor

they would also have been attended by the outstanding sons of nobles from other minor towns. Other buildings would have served as offices for government administration, law courts, markets, etc.

It is almost certain that, in accordance with their economic standing, craftsmen and farm laborers lived in the areas around these cities, in huts with palm-frond or straw-thatched rooves, similar to those still used today by a major portion of the rural population of Yucatán.

It is said that the ceremonial centers were accessible to the working and rural classes only on the occasion of great religious ceremonies, profane festivals, on market days and when they needed to solve some problem.

So as to better describe this site, it shall be divided into three sectors: (a) the North Group, consisting of various unrestored mounds, some of which are very large and which have not yet been named; (b) the Central Group, consisting of the extraordinary complex known as the Nunnery Quadrangle, the Pyramid of the Magician, the Ball Court, and the quadrangle known as the Cemetery Group; and (c) the South Group, consisting of the Governor's Palace, the House of the Turtles, the Great Pyramid, the Quadrangle of the Pigeons, plus, in back, another enormous pyramid, as yet unnamed and unrestored, and towards the southeast, the House of the Old Woman, who, according to the legend, was the mother of the dwarf magician; the latter house is almost joined to a medium-sized mound.

Aside from the above-mentioned buildings, there are a number of nearby mounds that have not been fully explored as yet, some of which have been named the Temple of the Phalluses, the House of Chimez and an arch in ruins, which marked the beginning of a white road, called "sac beh" in Maya, connecting Uxmal and Kabáh.

As the visitor approaches this fascinating archeological site, he can see almost directly in front of him and to the right, a series of unrestored mounds of different sizes which constitute the North Group; to his left, the impressive pyramid known as the Temple of the Magician, rises majestically. After the curve in the road, past the Hotel Hacienda Uxmal, the visitor should take the right-hand fork, so as to arrive at the only entrance. A tourist complex, to be inaugurated in the near future, is being built on the left-hand side.

After purchasing the admission ticket at the ticket office, the visitor will start his rounds at the restored cistern, just inside the entrance gates, and then continue on with the buildings described below.

THE CENTRAL GROUP

THE PYRAMID OF THE MAGICIAN.- This elliptic-shaped pyramid, a rather unusual shape, has been so named because it relates back to a legend that the Mayas of the Decadent Period still vividly remembered at the time of the conquest. The Spaniards must have been very impressed with it, as it was passed on down from generation to generation, to the point where, today, it is well-known to many Yucatecans and a considerable number of tourists, having been included in elementary school history books and in some guidebooks on Uxmal. Thus, when visitors ask about the origin of the name, it becomes necessary to tell the tale of the legend.

THE LEGEND OF THE DWARF MAGICIAN.- Many versions of this legend exist, with each author telling it somewhat differently, perhaps to make it more charming or interesting, but basically, it is as follows:

A few years prior to the final downfall of the Maya culture, Uxmal was governed by an ambitious and despotic sovereign, who was much hated by his subjects.

At that time, there was an old woman known to all as the "witch", who lived in a tiny hut on the outskirts of the community. She desperately wanted a child, but could no longer conceive because of her great age. One day, in a cave, she found a huge egg. She very carefully took it home with her, where she tried to keep it warm; during the day she would put it near the hearth and at night, she laid it on her breast. To her great surprise, a few days later, the egg hatched and a boy emerged, so small that he fit into the palm of her hand. He grew rapidly, but stopped growing when he was about three feet tall, and there he remained, a dwarf. This dwarf had extraordinary powers and could predict the future. He knew when the inhabitants of the region would have good crops or bad ones, he would predict hurricanes, plagues, epidemics, etc.; so they started calling him the "magician", and soon he became famous throughout the region.

The dwarf's mother had inherited a copper disk from her ancestors, which she kept hidden as she had been told to keep it a secret. So that no one would find it, she buried it in the earthen floor of the kitchen, and put the hearth over the hiding place. She frequently told her adored son never to go near the hearth, and not to even think about digging in its ashes. She said this so often, that the dwarf became suspicious and felt sure that something important was hidden there. One day, to keep his mother away from the house longer than usual, he made a number of holes in one of the jars that she used for carrying water. When the old woman noticed the holes, she sat down to repair them. Meanwhile, her son quickly removed the fire and dug into the floor underneath. Much to his surprise, he found the copper disk. He looked at it for a moment, and then picked it up and banged it against the floor with such force that the sound was heard for miles around. On hearing the sound, the hated monarch became very pensive and worried because, according to the prophesies and laws in effect at the time, he knew that he would have to turn over the reign of Uxmal, without any excuses, to the person that sounded the mysterious disk that could be heard throughout the region. The furious king ordered his soldiers to immediately find whoever had caused the sound, and to bring him into his presence. The soldiers asked around about the sound, and finally came to the witch's house, just as she was berating her son for his disobedience. Without considering his age, he was pushed and shoved into the presence of the monarch.

The people there knew of the prophecy, and followed the dwarf with great joy; they knew that their oppression would end when the tyrant was dethroned. The angry king looked at the dwarf and scornfully asked him why he had sounded the mysterious disk, to which the dwarf replied, "Because the time has come for you to hand your throne over to me, as the prophecy says." At first the king refused, but the people, who completely filled the plaza, started to shout in protest. To calm them down, the king said he would hand over the throne, if the dwarf could win three tests to which he would have to submit. The first test was that he had to guess the number of leaves on a huge tree that stood in the plaza; the second test was that both the dwarf and the king would each build an idol, and the idol that could withstand a fire would be the winner. The third and last test was that the dwarf would have one hundred "cocoyoles" (small fruit with nut) broken on his head, and if he was able to survive this, then the monarch would be submitted to the same test. A date was set, and the people were told to be there as witnesses.

The dwarf's mother was so worried that she could not sleep, and one day, while she was crying in the shade of a tree, a bat appeared to her. Nothing as enormous as that bat had ever been seen, and he said to her, "Don't worry, madam, your son will triumph in all the tests, if you do what I tell you to. Go to the cave where you found the egg, and there you will find a protective helmet covered by a wig, which will fit your son's head exactly. With that protective helmet he will be able to withstand the breaking of the cocoyoles without coming to harm. Tell him also to make his idol of clay, as the fire will not destroy it. I have found out that the king will make his from a very resistent stone, but he will fail. As to the tree, I will tell you how many leaves it has, but do not forget the number. I will take care of everything else." With that, the bat swiftly disappeared into the jungle.

The day of the tests dawned, and the people thronged the plaza; they were impatient for it all to begin, but they wondered about the dwarf's triumph because the tests were so difficult. In an arrogant and contemptuous tone, the king said to the child, "Miserable dwarf, you who say you can guess everything, tell me how many leaves there are on this tree." After thinking it over a few minutes, the dwarf, with aplomb, gave the figure his mother had told him. At that instant, the enormous bat made its appearance, and flying around the king, said, "The figure mentioned by the child is correct. I know, because I speak for the gods." And off it flew, leaving everyone agape.

Feeling much more hopeful, the people shouted jubilantly at the king that there was no need to count the leaves, that they believed the bat to be a messenger from the gods as animals do not otherwise talk. At first the king tried to resist, but the people persisted, and he finally had to give in.

During the second test, the king's idol, at first resisted the flames, but after a few hours, the stone split and shattered; the dwarf's idol, made of clay, withstood the heat perfectly.

In the last test, the dwarf survived the breaking of the cocoyoles on his head because of the protective helmet under the wig. When the king saw that only three cocoyoles were left, he tried to flee, but his soldiers, who also hated him, held him fast. When it was his turn to submit to the test, the first cocoyole that was broken on his head, smashed his skull and killed him.

So it was that the dwarf became the new monarch of Uxmal, reigning over his subjects with great wisdom from the temple that was built specifically for him, and which carries his name to this day.

We know that legends are fantasies that arise from peoples' imaginations, but sometimes there is a grain of truth in them.

Maybe there once had been a king at Uxmal, who was quite short and who had wisely governed his people, but he certainly was not born from an egg, nor did he undergo the difficult tests.

The Mayas, same as other Mesoamerican cultures, built their buildings at ground level, and after using them for a number of years, would cover them with thick layers of masonry and, for reasons unknown to us, build another structure on top of the original one. A number of researchers are of the opinion that these superimposed structures were made every 52 years, which is equal to one cycle of the Maya Round Calendar.

This contention is quite unacceptable because there are relatively few buildings in the ceremonial centers that have superimposed construction, and it is impossible that all of them were built just 52 years prior to the final downfall of the Maya culture. In addition, the wooden lintel found in the first substructure in the Temple of the Magician, indicated a date equivalent to 569 A.D., with a probable difference of 50 or so years (as has already been explained), and the latest explorations by the I.N.A.H. archeologists show that active life in Uxmal continued up to

Catherwood, the artist, found the east side of the Pyramid of the Magician in these conditions in 1841.

The second stage of restoration of the Pyramid of the Magician, under the direction of archaeologist, César Sáenz, in 1968-69. Photo taken from I.N.A.H. Bulletin No. 36. June 1969.

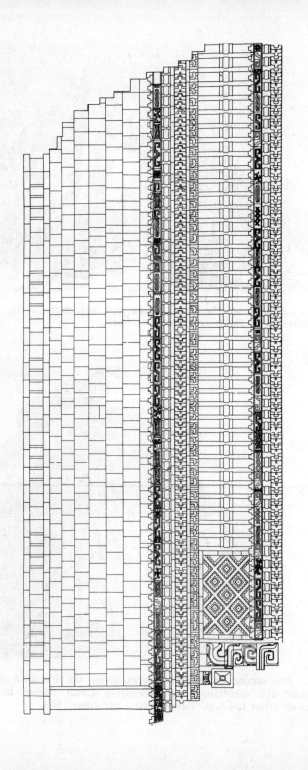

Drawing showing the condition of the rear portion of the first structure of the Pyramid of the Magician. Taken from I.N.A.H. Bulletin No. 36, June 1969.

Aerial photo of the Pyramid of the Magician and the Nunnery Quadrangle. Photo courtesy of José López Nájera.

the 12th Century, which coincides with the abandonment of Chichén Itzá in 1196. If, from that figure, we subtract the year 569 (from the lintel), we are left with 627 years; dividing this by 52, we get 12. If what the researchers believe is true, the Temple of the Magician would have 11 substructures. At Chichén Itzá, the North Group, which shows strong Toltec influence, is believed to have been started between 975 and 987 A.D., and abandoned in 1196. If we take the 209 year difference and divide it by 52, we get 4; however, in this sector, buildings of only one substructure have been found. All of the above should effectively refute the 52-year cycle theory.

Only five structure were known to exist in the Temple of the Magician, which happened to coincide with the five cycles. In 1968-69, however, César Saenz, an experienced and active I.N.A.H. archaeologists, dug a narrow tunnel through the east side of the first structure in this complex, and found its richly ornamented façade in very good condition. As the tunnel was too narrow to allow it to be photographed, he had an artist draw it; we offer the drawing in the foldout page.

During these same explorations, Mr. Saenz discovered evidence of another interior structure, which is why he believes that it represents at least six periods and not five, as was previously thought.

Mr. Saenz, on excavating the southern side of the base of this pyramid, found two sculptures in the debris, that appeared to represent what has been called the Queen of Uxmal; one of these is in the Anthropology Museum in Mérida. At the same site, he found three alike masks, sculpted in stone, with the smiling features of the god Tlaloc, similar to those made by the Teotihuacán people.

The main façade of the first structure of the Temple of the Magician faces west, and consists of five walled chambers, with an entrance door in each. The long cornice located over the doors, is decorated with different geometric designs done in relief; on top of this cornice are some small, round drums on which rest specially shaped circular stones; when these stones are put together, they form a long series of vertebrae. This cornice is duplicated along the back of the building, as can be seen from the foldout drawing.

Originally, over the central doorway and on top of the reliefs, there had been an embedded carving of a beautiful face with tattoos on the cheeks, and hair hanging down in a pageboy cut on either side of the face. This face appeared to emerge from the open mouth of a stylized serpent. That is the sculpture known as the Queen of Uxmal. Earlier this year it was torn from its base by the Mexican archeologist, Leopoldo Batres, who was head of the Historical Monuments Department of Mexico's archeological sites, and who took it to the National Museum of Anthropology in Mexico City, where it remains to this day.

Actually, this face does not appear to be female, its

features are rather masculine. One must remember that the Mayas almost never drew or sculpted women, as in that society they occupied a very secondary place.

After having used this first structure, the Mayas superimposed others. These were covered with a 22 meters tall, elliptic-shaped pyramid, on which three buildings were

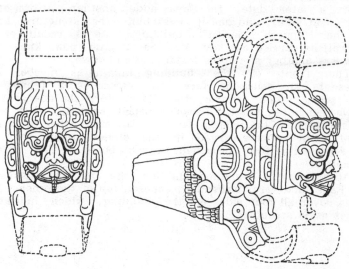

Drawings showing front and side views of one of two stone sculptures found in excavations carried out by Sáenz, on the south side of the Pyramid of the Magician, also published in the same Bulletin.

Mask of Tlaloc, found in the same excavation, Published in Bulletin No. 36.

The Queen of Uxmal. Drawing by Tatiana Proskouriakoff. Album of Maya Arcnitecture, p. 69.

built, as can be seen in the sketch.

The first of these three buildings, faces eastward and consists of three, small, narrow chambers that are connected to each other lengthwise. Subsequently, another structure was added, back to back with the first; its floor is slightly higher, and it consists of two chambers, one exterior and one interior; the latter is the narrower one.

At a later date, the Mayas added another platform at the front (west side), and on it was built the structure known as the "fourth period" building. As a result of the explorations carried out by Mr. Saenz, we now know that there was another structure inside, possibly two.

The front of the building known as number four, represents an enormous face that resembles a feline; the open jaws, wider towards the floor, form the door. Above the wooden lintel, small, diamond-shaped squares were added to represent the feline's teeth. To make the face more realistic, curves were carved in the stones under each eye to represent the prominent cheek bones. The nose is incomplete.

All around the building and on the corners, masks of the Rain God are embedded, one on top of the other. Many reliefs cover all four sides of the building, which indicate a Chenes style structure.

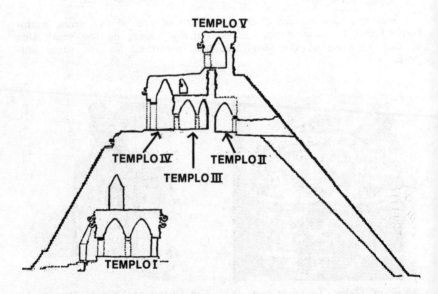

Sketch showing the superimposed buildings of the Pyramid of the Magician, as they were originally. From the .I.N.A.H. Official Guide to Uxmal, p. 7, July 15, 1959.

Parallel to the stairs on this side, there are twelve masks with long, upward-curving noses, and spiraled eyes (perhaps they are meant to represent crossed eyes). The stairs are 8.15 meters wide and almost 22 meters high.

After the Mayas used these last structures, they covered the buildings known as two and three, shown on the sketch, with the last elliptic-shaped platform, on top of which they

This is how Catherwood, the artist, saw the west side of the Pyramid of the Magician in the 1841.

West side of the fourth superimposed structure of the Pyramid of the Magician. Photo courtesy of Francisco Góngora.

Aerial view of the Nunnery Quadrangle and the Pyramid of the Magician. Photo courtesy of José López Nájera.

placed another rectangular platform. And on top of that, they erected the building known as the House of the Magician.

Archeologists were able to find the structure shown as number two, because of the tunnel that was excavated at the level of the first elliptic-shaped platform, where a high stairway, 30 meters high and with 118 steps, was also found. This eastern side is the back of the Temple of the Magician.

THE NUNNERY QUADRANGLE

About 70 meters west of the Temple of the Magician, are a series of incredibly beautiful buildings that form a quadrangle. The stone filigrees capture the most outstanding aspects of the exterior sculptural art practiced by those ancient architects.

We are almost positive that nowhere in Pre-Colombian America is there another complex as magnificent as this. The name of "Nunnery Quadrangle" was given by the Franciscan friar, Diego López de Cogolludo, because the buildings reminded him of the religious convents in Spain.

Some researchers believe that these buildings were the living quarters of the nobles who ruled the Mayas of the region. This author believes that these marvellous buildings functioned as an educational center, since people without education or professional training could not have built such buildings. They were undoubtedly the work of talented engineers and architects who had to have an appropriate place in which to house and teach their arts and sciences. The chambers do appear to be rather small, but at that time, the number of people who had the privilege of learning, was relatively small; perhaps there were no more than 12 or 15 students per class or subject.

Given the economics and customs in effect at that time, apprenticeship in a profession consisted of learning only two or three subjects directly related to it; thus, in a short time, studies were completed and they were considered experts in their field, although they knew little or nothing of anything else.

Although the front chambers are somewhat dark now because of the humidity, at the time they were in use, they were probably whitewashed and therefore, lighter. The interior, darker chambers, may have been used as storerooms for educational materials and implements, or they may have been used by the priests who did the teaching, as retreats for spiritual rest and meditation.

This complex of buildings is about three meters higher than the level of the central plaza. Each building sits at a different level, which leads us to believe that the entire complex was not planned at the same time; however, on

41

Partial view of the Nunnery Quadrangle. Photo by the author.

erecting each addition, the builders were very careful not to jeopardize the esthetic feeling of the whole.

Some years ago, a hole was dug in the rear platform of the western building, which clearly allowed us to see the upper part of an arch and some of the stones used to seal it. This hole was covered when the Light and Sound Show installations were put in. This tells us two things: firstly, that the western building was built over an existing structure, and secondly, that the quadrangular patio was lowered to its present level.

If the visitor is observant, he will note that the floors of the eastern and western buildings are of the same height and that this height also coincides with the level of the central cornice of the southern building. He will also note that the roof of this southern building coincides with the level of the central cornices of the eastern and western buildings, as well as with the platform of the building on the northern side. This combination gives the whole complex a most appealing aspect.

Another important characteristic of the Maya architecture, which few have noted, is that the majority of their buildings are sloped slightly forwards, and no one has been able to satisfactorily explain why. At first, this author assumed that this slope served as a counterweight to the angle of the false arch, as can be seen in the following drawing; but subsequently, we noted that the upper part of the façade of the Palace at Kabah, and the upper part of the Nunnery at Chichén Itzá, slope in the opposite direction, or backwards, so as to simulate the palm-frond or straw-thatched roofs of the huts of the poor.

The late Yucatecan archeologist, Manuel Cirerol Sansores, believed that the purpose of this slope was to make the reliefs stand out more at certain hours of the day. Most probably, however, the Maya architects tried to demonstrate their creative genius by defying gravity as much as possible.

EAST SIDE OF THE QUADRANGLE.- The building on this side is 48 meters long and 10.50 meters wide; it is 8.50 meters high, and has five doors or entrances. Its decoration consists of six trapezoids outlined with serpent's heads. These heads are placed one on top of the other, on an outward slant; however, the bottom ones jut out less than the top ones so as to compensate for the slant of the façade; had this not been done the serpent's heads would slant forwards.

In the upper center of each trapezoid, is a human face, beautifully carved in relief. As these faces are covered with designs that look like small feathers, some researchers have thought them to be owls, which cannot be because they have noses instead of beaks. Along the upper cornice there are, equidistantly placed, fringed rosettes. The rest of the façade, between the upper and central cornices, is decorated with exes or crosses which, on being joined form a stone lattice. Over the central door, and at each end of the building, there are three superimposed masks of the so-called rain god. At each end of the upper cornice, a serpent head is embedded, and at each end of the central cornice, there is a tortoise head. The central chamber has two small inside passages, one on the left and one on the right.

It is quite probable that this whole building complex had originally been painted in various colors. In the trapezoid at the far left, one can still clearly see the original red of the background; and greenish blue spots are still visible on

Drawing of the technique used by the Mayas in building their false arch.

the eyebrows of the two upper serpents. Just imagine, dear reader, how magnificent this must have looked in its time of splendor!

During the Light and Sound Show, when the lights shine on the reliefs causing stark shadows, the visitor can really appreciate the precision with which the figures, lines and architectural details have been cut in these majestic buildings.

SOUTH SIDE OF THE QUADRANGLE.- This side is the least decorated; it also sits at the lowest level. Its decoration consists of repeated designs all along its 53 meter length; it is 5.70 meters high. This is the only building that has two rows of chambers, that is, there are eight

This is how the East side and part of the North Side looked in the Nunnery Quadrangle prior to restoration. Photo on p.22, of the book "Arquitectura Precolombina de México" by Manuel Amábilis Dominguez.

East side of the Nunnery Quadrangle after restoration. Photo by the author.

chambers, with a door or entrance in each, facing the front, and another eight facing south with their respective doors. The upper cornice had been decorated with fringed rosettes, much like those on the east building; the restorers, when they could not find the rosettes, left the holes to show where they had been embedded. Over each door, a straw-thatched hut was carved with a hollow square for the door. Over each hut are the only rain god masks that we have seen without long noses; the trunk-like noses were replaced with a cone-shaped triangle and a small corn-cob. To

This is how Catherwood saw the South side of the Nunnery Quadrangle. Note the condition of the patio.

Side view of the same South side after restoration. Photo by the author.

embellish the façade, a latticework of exes or crosses had been added. In the center of this building, as the main entrance to this group, there is an arched passageway that leads outside. The vault of the arch had been covered with stucco and paintings had been added, some vestiges of which can still be seen. After the stucco had fallen off from various sections, red-painted hands were visible on the walls. It is said they are symbolic representations of the hands of the high priest Itzamná, founder and governor of Chichén Itzá, who introduced architecture, arts and sciences to the Yucatán Peninsula, and who became a deity upon his death.

WEST SIDE OF THE QUADRANGLE.- This side appears to be the most decorated, and was also the most destroyed, as can be seen by the drawings made by the English architect and artist, Frederick Catherwood, who visited Uxmal with Mr. John L. Stephens for the first time in 1840; this visit was interrupted by Catherwood's almost dying from a malaria attack. They returned in 1841, wiser and more careful. At that time, they carried out much more detailed studies, and this master of brush and pencil, made some magnificent drawings of buildings at various sites throughout the Maya region. These drawings were so perfect that some rivaled even the best photographs taken today. We have included some of these in this guidebook, so that the reader may see the conditions of some of these buildings, prior to restoration.

View of the West side of the Quadrangle after restoration. Photo by the author.

Two sections of the west side of the Nunnery Quadrangle prior to restoration. Drawing by Catherwood.

Corner of the West side of the Nunnery Quadrangle. Photo by the author.

Another detail of the same facade. Photo by the author.

Detail of the center portion of the same facade. Photo by the author.

The visitor can see that along three sides of this quadrangle, the building doors are wider and the decorations over the doors are rather special, probably to show that this was the most important portion. And so as not to lose their esthetic appeal, the entrances to the chambers always add up to odd numbers (the main entrance being formed by the arch on the south side, as already explained).

The building on the west side is 53 meters long and 10.50 meters wide; there are seven interior chambers and seven exterior chambers with seven doors. The interior chambers are mostly in ruins, but it is obvious that they had no outlets towards the rear of the building. At each end of the façade, there are three superimposed masks of the rain god. Starting at the right corner and going left, one can see over the first door, a straw-thatched hut worked in stone, over which there is a large mask. Further to the left, in the center of a fret, there is a figure of a naked man embedded, with tattoed thighs and genitals. Next to him, is the head of an open-mouthed serpent from which a human face projects. It is generally believed that the serpent is not swallowing the man, but bringing him into the world; perhaps that is why this reptile is considered to be the symbol of fertility.

The body of the serpent winds downwards, then it disappears behind a stack of three more large masks and then reappears and intertwines with the body of another serpent that is coming from the opposite direction. On intertwining, their bodies wind upwards, but before reaching the upper cornice, they separate. The serpent with the open mouth goes back to the right, and after a short disappearance, appears again and ends with the rattles of its tail pointing at its neck. Over the tail, there is a lovely cup from which a tuft of feathers protrudes, as can be seen in the following photographs.

The people who planned the Light and Sound Show, perhaps to impress the spectators, made a mistake in illuminating this snake, because instead of turning back, the light shines on the other snake and picks up on the tail at the far left (south side). It is almost certain that the snake that was described above was added to the building at a later date, which is why it is interrupted and why some of the original reliefs are damaged. One must also remember, that the concept of the feathered serpent was brought by the Toltecs, long after this structure had been built.

Above the central doorway, there is a small platform with finely-chiseled reliefs, and on it stands the " turtle Man", thus named because he has the body of a turle and the head of a man. Next to it is another oval stone shaped like a turtle's carapace and engraved with the small figure of a man in a boxer's stance. Next to that, is the "Bat Man", surrounded by an oval flower with pointed petals; this figure was so named because both the eyes and the ears resemble those of a vampire bat. The next figure embedded in the wall has a serious expression on his face and is holding what appears to be a scroll of paper in his hands; the ribbon that is holding his cape is tied in a knot on one side of his chest. Maybe he represents one of the professors here, if this was an educational center, as has already been postulated.

NORTH SIDE OF THE QUADRANGLE.- The building here is the longest and highest of the quadrangle; it is 83 meters long and 10.50 meters wide. It has eleven doors along the front, with each giving into a double chamber; the interior chambers have no outlet to the rear of the building. At each end, there is another chamber, with its respective door.

The visitor will note that from the center towards the left and up to the fifth door, the reliefs are almost intact, but the opposite side is almost empty except for a row of superimposed masks towards the last door, plus another row at the corner of that same side. Between the two rows of masks, the figure of an owl can be found, embedded in the center of a fret.

Above the central door, there is another row of masks; and over the next door is a straw-thatched hut carved in stone. This hut used to have three serpent's heads on each side of the roof, but one has been lost. These decorations are repeated to the end of the building, over the fifth door.

An observant person will note that each large mask of the so-called rain god is different. Some researchers believe these masks to be faces of the "sacred serpent", although none actually looks like one. The masks at the southwest corner of the east building are stylized faces of old men; and the three masks located over the second door on the northern side of the west building, when illuminated by the Light and Sound Show, are clearly children's faces.

From the photograph taken of the north side of this

This is how the North side of the Nunnery Quadrangle looked prior to restoration. Photo from p. 135 of the book "Arquitectura Precolombina de México" by Manuel Amábilis Domínguez.

The same North side of the Quadrangle after restoration. Photo by the author.

Detail of the same North side, showing a straw-thatched hut carved in stone. Photo by the author.

quadrangle prior to restoration, one can see the extent of the damage to this building. On restoring and fixing this building, the archeologists could not find the stones for the reliefs, although this was not the case on the west side, where the buildings were actually in worse shape. I often wondered where those stones might have ended up after the building fell in ruins. After much reflection, I remembered an anecdote published by the late Dr. Eduardo Ursaiz Rodríguez, under the pseudonym Claudio Mex, in his fascinating book entitled "Anécdotas Yucatecas - Reconstrucción de Hechos" (Yucatecan Anecdotes - Reconstruction of Facts). On page 10, he says the following: "Before the Maya ruins became the property of the State, the owner of Uxmal, Simón Peón, used the carved stones in building the water troughs on his ranch. In talking with Stephens in 1841, and on asking him to admire the solidity of the buildings, he said: 'If I had these ruins in New Orleans, I'd make a fortune selling stones.' 'Oh!,' answered Stephens, 'you could make a fortune putting a fence around them and charging a peseta for people to come and see them.'" This anecdote made me think that Simón Peón used the stones from the ruined buildings at Uxmal not only to build water troughs, but also to build houses and fences. From other sources, we know that Peón gave Stephens permission to take away some carved stones, with the exception of the serpent heads described in the west building, as he intended to put them up somewhere in his house in Mérida. That is one reason why, in some instances, the total restoration of a building becomes impossible.

The front of the northern building described above, has a simple, but well-proportioned stairway, 28 meters wide, which leads to the floor of the quadrangle's patio. Before reaching the floor, however, there is a throne or seat, in the center, totally covered with complicated and enigmatic hieroglyphs that are quite eroded, but that perhaps, could give some explanations on this marvellous complex. At the patio level, and on either side of this stairway, there are two structures, consisting of double chambers - one in front and one in the back. The chambers on the east side could not be completely restored, possibly because not all the original materials were found; however, the west side structure is almost complete. Along the front, the roof is supported by two small wall panels on either side, the remainder being supported by four, short grooved columns with beautifully decorated bases and capitals. The façade is simple, consisting of five horizontal rectangles divided in the center as if they represented eyes in a face; the rest is covered with diamond-shaped dentated stones. The cornice had pretty, decorative rosettes at equidistant intervals along it, but some are missing now.

One guidebook on Uxmal, calls this building the "Temple of Venus", without specifying the reason for this name.

In a report published in an I.N.A.H. bulletin not too long ago, it says that, according to Kubler, a date found on a wood lintel from the north building is equivalent to the year 893 A.D., plus or minus 100 years. However, the Groningen laboratory gives a much earlier date, 653 A.D., plus or minus 100 years, from another piece of wood from the same building. It is also believed that this north building is the oldest in the quadrangle. This author is inclined to believe this latter (or earlier) date, because it coincides with what has already been said regarding the time at which Uxmal was occupied. A simple analysis, tells us that the north side could not have been the oldest because of the substructure that exists on the west side; on the other hand, the highest building must logically have been built at a later date.

The visitor that has seen the magnificence of this impressive architectural complex, which is doubtless one of the most significant works of art of the ancient cultures of this continent, will take back unforgettable memories of the grandness of Uxmal and its buildings.

THE BALL COURT.- About 100 meters south of the above quadrangle, and towards the Governor's Palace, there is a small ball court, almost totally in ruins; however, about four years ago, the debris was cleared and some restoration began to take place.

The ball game was played in similar fashion by almost all the Mesoamerican cultures, and even by some primitive tribes in Arizona, U.S.A., where an enormous ball court exists, with parallel walls and embedded rings.

Tatiana Proskouriakoff's version of How the Nunnery Quadrangle and the Pyramid of the magician could have looked in their times of splendor. Drawing No. 18 in her "Album of Maya Architecture". Fondo de Cultura Económica, México, 1958.

Some researchers believe that this game was invented in Teotihuacán for the entertainment of the gods, kings and priests; and that from there, it spread to other cultures, particularly the Mesoamerican ones. Even though the ball courts are similar to each other, each culture built them with their own characteristics. One of the largest known is at Chichén Itzá, which still clearly shows reliefs of seven players per team carved on the lateral walls. Nevertheless, other, smaller ball courts have been uncovered at that site that show a different number of players.

The ball court at Uxmal, consists of two, thick, parallel walls, about 25 meters long, and with a 12 meter space between the walls. At the center of these walls, as in all ball courts, one can still see parts of the stone rings through which the rubber ball was supposedly thrown. Some hieroglyphs around the edges of these rings, can still be made out.

Running along the upper front part of the walls are the characteristic platforms, which almost all the ball courts have (in some instances, slanted forwards). Along the ground, are the sections of some feathered serpents that used to be part of the wall ornamentation. On the west side wall, one can still see the end of a serpent's tail with its rattles. On the top of these wide walls, are the foundations of some narrow chambers.

The late archaeologist, Eric S. Thompson, to whom we owe much of the knowledge on the ancient Mayas, believed that the hieroglyphics on one of the stone rings indicated the date 649 A.D. If this date is really correct, we do not believe that it indicates the age of the building, because both the feathered serpent and the slope along the rear, are

In the foreground, two small mounds showing the actual condition of the Ball Court; in the rear, the Nunnery Quadrangle. Photo by de author.

typically Toltec. There is no doubt that this ball court was contemporary to the one at Chichén Itzá. One must also remember that, at most, only one-third of one ring and one-fourth of another ring still exist -- perhaps, the numbers researched do not refer to dates.

THE CEMETERY GROUP.- At this site, the inhabitants adopted the system of erecting their buildings around quadrangles, as in the Nunnery Quadrangle, described above.

West of the Ball Court, there is another, unrestored quadrangle, which has been named the "Cemetery Group", solely because in the center there are four small platforms, asymetrically shaped, with reliefs of skulls and crossbones. At the corners of some of these, the skulls are properly head-shaped; others are stylized, with what appear to be turbans and small bones at each side of the jaws. Mysterious hieroglyphs, that serve as frames of the upper part, complete the reliefs.

A pyramid, destroyed to the point where it seems to be a natural mound, is found at the north side of the quadrangle.

On the west side, on top of an elevated platform, there is a house, about 10 meters long. Its roof, instead of sloping forwards like in the other buildings, slopes backwards, possibly so that it would resemble the straw-thatched huts. On top of it there is an ornamental superstructure, which archeologists call a "crest", when it rests on the upper part of the façade as this does; when it is level with the front wall, it is called a false façade.

The experts tell us that this ornamental system was used

Detail of the reliefs carved in one of the Cemetery Group's platforms. Photo by the author.

by the Mayas approximately between the years 600 and 800 BC, and that its function was to make the buildings look taller and more impressive. The holes served to protect the crest from the wind during heavy tropical storms, making the wall less heavy and providing a better appearance. At Tikal, in Guatemala, these crests and false façades are sometimes twice as high as the buildings themselves.

Along the south and east sides of this quadrangle, long mounds can be seen that were probably rows of chambers that have toppled down.

We are almost certain that this complex was not a cemetery; more probably, it was a place where funerals were held for the nobles who died, using the various platforms according to their hierarchical order, and from which they were taken to the real cemetery or to be cremated. We know that the Mayas used cremation, particularly for their nobles, as clay vessels, containing ashes, pieces of burnt bone, and some times offerings, have been found upon excavating some buildings.

SOUTH GROUP

THE GOVERNOR'S PALACE.- Because of its size, enormous proportions, ornamentation and construction techniques, this building is considered to be the single most important at Uxmal, and one of the most remarkable in this hemisphere from the Pre-Hispanic era. Sylvanus G. Morley, the noted U.S. archaeologists, had the stones counted that were decorating the façade on all four sides, and concluded that it consisted of 20,000 pieces. It is quite possible, that he had the front and one side counted, then doubled the number to arrive at the total, because the rear of the building is incomplete.

This palace sits on three superimposed platforms. The first is an enormous, rectangular terrace that is 12 meters high. The front is 180 meters long, and the north and south sides are 150 meters long. The second platform is much smaller, being seven meters high, with the front and back 120 meters long, and the sides 27 meters long. The last platform is only one meter high and 100 meters long. It has been calculated that these three platforms have an earth volume of half a million cubic meters.

So that the exterior of the first and second terraces would look more beautiful, the Maya architects added narrow, superimposed platforms that were covered with flat stones, some of which are still in their original settings. Access to the palace was provided by a wide staircase located on the east side of the first terrace. This stairway is in ruins and covered with vegetation; not so the one on the second terrace, which has been totally restored.

The palace itself is 97.5 meters long, 12 meters wide and 8 meters high. Originally, the building had 20 chambers, but the arched passageways that gave access to the rear

This is how the great artist Catherwood saw the Governor's Palace in 1841.

The Governor's Palace today. Photo by the author.

were closed off; each arch was then converted into two chambers, bringing the total to 24.

The façade is decorated with a series of repeated motifs. To the left of the right arch, on the corner, there are five large masks between the upper and central cornices. At the level of the bottom mask and to the left, there are five more large masks which stairstep upwards; six large masks run below the upper cornice, then five masks stairstep downwards again. This sequence is repeated to cover the entire façade. Between these alike masks, frets were placed in combination with a series of square stones; the remainder was covered with exes to form delicate latticework friezes. To beautify the building even more, an ondulating serpent was carved along the upper cornice, which wraps around all four sides of the structure. The three central doors (with the middle one being the widest) open on to a long chamber, behind which there is another identical chamber, except it has only one door in the center.

The ornamentation over this central door is unique. Two sides of a trapezoid are formed by serpents' heads, and in the middle is an incomplete idol that is sitting on a horseshoe-shaped throne; its head, forearms, one thigh, and the legs are missing. Over where its head would have been, is a lovely tuft of feathers. Along horizontal grooves, at the level of the serpent's heads, are lines of hieroglyphs which might possibly explain something about this building.

The Franciscan friar, Diego López de Cogolludo is attributed with naming this building the Governor's Palace because he considered it an administration building. We are in agreement with the cleric, because the Mayas must have had an almost perfect administrative organization, and a building in which to house it, to have accomplished their

The House of the Turtles. Drawing by Catherwood.

The House of the Turtles prior to its latest restoration. Photo by A. Cabrera, courtesy of Irma Cantón de Cárdenas.

The house of the Turtles today. Photo by the author.

majestic works of art.

By the photographs in this guidebook, the reader will get a good idea of what this building looked like, before and after its restoration. When Stephens visited Uxmal in 1841, he found out from the owner, Simón Peón, that in 1825, the destroyed portion (which we show in the drawing made prior to restoration) was in place, and that the whole frontispiece was almost intact.

In front of this palace and in the center of a low, square platform, is an enormous, almost cylindrical, tilted monolith which resembles a phallic symbol.

On exploring other buildings, various of these symbols have been found; they are about 60 cms high and have a diameter of about 25 cms. The Mayas revered them, considering them the element that initiates life.

A few steps away from this enormous monolith, is a square platform, about one meter high, with stairs on all four sides. In the center, rests the statue of a two-headed animal, each head facing away from the other; this is assumed to be a jaguar, although the heads appear to be more puma-like, with bared fangs. Even today, the Mayas call the puma "coh", which means teeth, because this animal is known to bare its teeth, particularly when angry. When Stephens excavated the small mound that covered this platform, he found the statue. Simón Peón took it to another of his properties, but it was returned to its place of origin when the platform was restored.

THE HOUSE OF THE TURTLES.- At the northeast corner of the enormous platform or terrace of the Governor's Palace, there is a building which has been named the House of the Turtles, because along its upper cornice and all around the building, some beautifully sculpted turtles have been embedded. They are symmetrically distributed and of different sizes, and have varied reliefs carved on their carapaces. For the Mayas, turtles represent one of the main elements of life, that is, water or the beneficient rain, from which their livelihood depended. The sculptors who carved these turtles were truly masters, as they are unbelievably realistic.

This structure is 30 meters long, east to west, 11 meters wide, north to south, and about seven meters high. It is divided into three sections: in the central portion, it has three square chambers joined to each other lengthwise. The chamber on the south side, recently restored, has three doors, while the chamber on the north side has only one. Both chambers connect with the middle one by means of one door. The central and north chambers are still roofless. On each side there are two double chambers, one in front and one in back; the former has three doors, the latter only one. There is a low, masonry platform in the front chamber, which could have been a bench, a bed or an altar.

The ornamentation on this building is rather simple compared to the sumptuousness of the Governor's Palace. On all four sides, between the upper and central cornices, narrow, vertical columns have been embedded. Both cornices consist of two molded bands with a fillet or listel in the center.

So that the reader will have an idea of how this building

looked in 1841, we are reproducing a drawing by the great artist Catherwood, whom we have already mentioned.

If a visitor is lucky enough to visit Uxmal on a sunny afternoon, and be standing on this platform when the setting sun sheds its orange light on the impressive Pyramid of the Magician and the lavish Nunnery Quadrangle, he shall marvel at the grandiosity and majesty of this incomparable archeological site, and remember it forever.

THE GREAT PYRAMID.- At the southwest corner of the Governor's Palace, is a pyramid of huge proportions, and only because of that, it was named the Great Pyramid.

Until early 1972, it was covered with rubble and vegetation, and only a small section of the top building's façade was visible. Dr. Morley, whom we have already mentioned, once said that if he had a million pesos, he would have it restored. But it was only in September of 1972, that the I.N.A.H. began to carry out the restoration work, and the distinguished and active archaeologists, César Sáenz, was asked to head up the work.

In our opinion, César Sáenz is an extraordinary archeologist who works quickly and with a real sense of responsibility. In fact, this Great Pyramid was magically converted from a pile of rubble in only eight months and with only 24 workers (Maya masons and laborers) to what one sees today. The reader will be able to follow the progress of the work carried out, by the photographs shown here. We are also

Secuence of restoration, in 1972-73, of the Great Pyramid by archaeologist Cesar Sáenz of the I.N.A.H. of México. Photos by the author.

A)

most grateful to Mr. Sáenz, who kindly and generously answered all the questions we asked him during the exploration and restoration work, not only at this pyramid, but also at other sites in the Puuc area.

This pyramid is over 30 meters high, and its base is 100 meters long and 70 meters wide; it is very probable that it

B)

C)

rests on other substructures.

If we look at the eastern side of this building, we can see a bore hole that was made during research activities, through which can be seen the side wall of the building that crowns this pyramid. One can also see that this monument was being covered, to add another structure on top, when

D)

E)

this site was abandoned. We came to this conclusion, when we saw that the eastern side was covered not only with rubble, but also with masonry work. Aside from this, the façades of the other sides do not appear to be very destroyed, so it seems that the amount of rubble that covers them could not have come from this building. The front of

F)

G)

the building that crowns this structure is quite long; in the center there are some narrow, walled-up chambers that were added at a later date, which is why they jut out. The whole front façade is in the Chenes style, its decoration starting at floor level. Although the upper part is totally in ruins, it is possible that it was decorated in the same manner.

The ornamentation of this central portion consists of panels bordered with a succession of exes that may represent two intertwined and stylized serpents. Inside the panels are frets, and between one fret and another, there are some peculiar parrots. Some parrots have spread wings and separated legs and are facing forwards; some have their heads turned to the left, others to the right, and still others face forwards; some are horizontal, as if in flight, and others are head downwards. There must have been some reason for representing them this way, although we do not know what it might have been.

At either side of this out-jutting portion, there are numerous panels with reliefs of frets, rosettes and human faces that remind us of the Olmecs. These faces are surrounded by four and seven-pointed stars, with inter-laced filaments. On both the left and right corners, there are three large masks with long noses, which are different from the others that are characteristic of this region -- from the triangular mouth of each of these deities, a human face emerges, and on either side of the nose, there are very pronounced phallic symbols.

To get to the top of this pyramid, one must climb 66 steps, interrupted by a rest area or landing. At either side of the rest area, steps continue upwards to another landing, then comes the low platform on which this building sits. There are four, narrow steps from the platform to the level of the building. Another platform, possibly for ceremonial use, juts out in the center of the stairway after the first landing.

At either side of this high and wide staircase, there are nine superimposed platforms; the same number as in the Castle or Temple of Kukulcán at Chichén Itzá.

It is a pity that the restoration work was not continued so that we could know if the other sides were the same as the front.

THE QUADRANGLE OF THE PIGEONS.- West of the Great Pyramid, is another quadrangle bordered on all four sides by long rows of chambered buildings, although they are almost totally in ruins. On the east side, next to the base of the Great Pyramid, one can see vestiges of one such row of chambers; the same can be seen on the west side, and on the south side, where another enormous, unrestored pyramid is located. We can get an idea of what this architectural complex may have looked like from the north-facing, front portion which also seems to have been the most important building. This section has a long wall that was the central divider for 16 chambers, eight facing inwards, and eight outwards, of which only a portion of the vaulted arches remain. Over this wall and at roof level, there is a long, narrow wall with a series of small square windows, spaced at about one meter intervals. Over these little windows, there is a three-banded cornice, and on top of this, equally spaced along its entire length, are nine, tall triangles. These triangles consist of horizontal lines of small square openings that become successively shorter towards the top, so as to form the triangles. In the centers of these triangles, are some flat stones that jut out, which probably held idols, like at the Governor's Palace.

Because these lines of small openings resemble pigeon

The House of the Pigeon Photo by the author.

this building is considered unique in the whole Maya area.

It is appropriate here to mention another person who has contributed much to the work done with respect to the Mayas: Tatiana Proskouriakoff who emigrated from Russia to the United States in 1916, and who became a U.S. citizen holes, this building was named the Pigeon House, although there is no relationship whatsoever to these small birds. In another part of this book, we have already explained the function of the openings in the ornamental crests and false façades.

After visiting this site, Stephens noted that in this building he had seen stucco figures and decorations, which led him to assume that it was thus ornamented. In the center of this north side there is a vaulted arch which was the main entrance to this quadrangle.

Because of its extreme length, the ornamental crest of

when she turned 15. Subsequently, she studied drawing, architecture, and anthropology, the latter at the University of Pennsylvania.

In 1939, she went to work as an artist at the Research and History Division of the Carnegie Institution in Wash-

Tatiana Proskouriacoff's version of how the Quadrangle of the Pigeons could have looked in its time of splendor. Drawing No. 20 in her "Album of Maya Architecture".

ington, D.C. Later, she became a researcher at Harvard University's Peabody Museum. By that time, she had already combined her theoretical studies with practical ones, by going on a University of Pennsylvania expedition to Piedras Negras, in Guatemala. In 1939, she went to Copán, Honduras; in 1939 and 1940 she went to Chichén Itzá; and from 1951 to 1955, she collaborated in preparing the complicated map of Mayapán, and in excavations being carried out there by the Carnegie Institution. Between 1960 and 1963, with the expertise acquired during her many years of important work, she published three magnificent books on the ancient Maya, with particular emphasis on epigraphy; these books were widely acclaimed by the critics experts in this field.

Tatiana Proskouriakoff's most notable contributions were her speculative drawings of how various important buildings from different Maya sites would look when restored. These were published, together with many interesting and important descriptions, in her magnificent book "An Album of Maya Architecture". As basis for this imaginary restoration work, Proskouriakoff used the scant architectural details that were still visible in the ruined monuments. Incredibly, when some of these buildings were actually restored, they bore astounding resemblance to her drawings. The point of all this is that in the building known as the Quadrangle of the Pigeons, she not only visualized the restoration as it was subsequently done and described above, but she also showed the existence of a substructure beneath the front terrace of this north building, which consisted of three chambers followed by a staircase that went up to the roof which, in turn, was part of the front terrace of the House of the Pigeons. On the far left of this substructure, she showed another row of chambers jutting out towards the front. With this information, this author explored the area, and found the substructure. The front portion is totally in ruins, but portions of the arches on the opposite side are still standing; proof of the staircase was also found.

It is truly unfortunate that this building, as well as other important structures at Uxmal, are almost totally and continually covered by dense vegetation.

K A B A H

The significance of the name of this important archeological site has caused some interpretive controversies, as this Maya word has different meanings. If we pronounce it all in one breath, it means name, but it would have been absurd for the Mayas of the Decadent Period to name in "name". If we divide it into two words, we have "kab" which means hand (present-day Mayas do not pronounce the b), and "bah" which has two meanings. The first is mole (the rodent that lives in tunnels in the ground and feeds on plant roots), and the second is to drive into or insert, which is why a Yucatecan anthropologist, who died a few years ago and who spoke quite a lot of Maya, interpreted the name as "the hand that sculpts", even though there is considerable difference between sculpting and driving something into something. This author believes that Kabah means "the hand of the mole", which is a name that may have been given to the site by the Mayas of the Decadent Period, long after it had been abandoned.

In trying to find the meaning of this name, it occurred to me that the Mayas that lived in the nearby village of Santa Elena, which, prior to the Spaniard's arrival, had been called Nohcacab ("noh" meaning big, and "cacab" meaning fertile earth), frequently visited the ruined sites of their ancestors, and on one occasion, when digging around in the rubble, they could have found a stone or tile with a carving of a mole's hand or paw. On wishing to go to the site again, they would say to each other, "Let's go to the place where we found the mole's hand." With the passage of time, the name would have stayed.

Some time ago, I had a group of Spanish-speaking tourists at Kabah, and while we were waiting for a persistent drizzle to end, someone in the group asked me about the meaning of the name. I told them more or less what I have described above, but while doing so, I noticed that the man who has been the guard here for almost 30 years, Patricio Salazar, was paying unusual attention to my story. When I finished, he surprised me by saying that I was absolutely correct in what I had surmised. I asked him how come he knew that, and he told me that some years before, when the highway was still unpaved, a German tourist had come to buy a ticket. This German spoke Spanish and had asked Salazar why this place had been named Kabah. Salazar replied that he did not know why, that the name had been given during the Decadent Period and had since just been handed down. The foreigner replied that it was ironic that someone from the area would not know why, when he, a stranger, did. Salazar was surprised and asked the man how that was possible. The German said, "Many years ago, when this highway still didn't exist, I came here, on horseback, with a friend to explore the site. Among the rubble of one of the ruins, we found a stone slab, about 30 cms long and 20 cms wide, which had a low-relief carving of a hand on it, the fingers were hanging downwards, and drops of blood were dropping from the ends of the claws. I'll draw you a picture, if you like, so you can see what I mean."

To prove what he had said, Salazar went to fetch the drawing, which was as he had described it. He had asked the foreigner what had happened to the relief, and was told that it had been taken to a machine shop in Mérida, to have part of it removed so as to make it lighter, and that it was now in his private collection.

So from the telling of this tale, dear reader, you can see how from speculation and coincidence, the truth emerged.

Kabah is located 22 kilometers southwest of Uxmal, along the "Via Larga" highway, which goes to the city of Campeche. It is a medium-sized archeological site, covering about 1.5 kms from

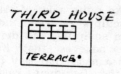

THIRD HOUSE

TERRACE•

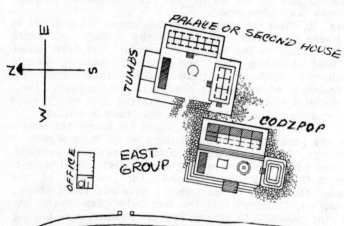

PALACE OR SECOND HOUSE

TUMBS

CODZPOP

EAST GROUP

OFFICE

N
E
W
S

Sketch of Kabah.

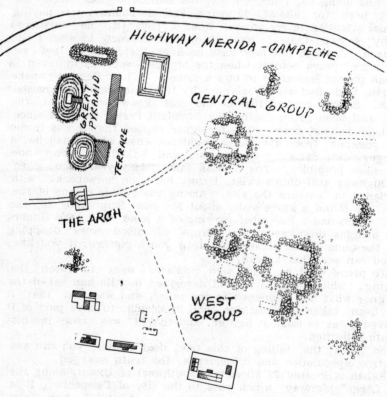

HIGHWAY MERIDA - CAMPECHE

GREAT PYRAMID

TERRACE

CENTRAL GROUP

THE ARCH

WEST GROUP

east to west and about 750 meters from north to south. It is divided into three groups of buildings, as can be seen from the sketch we provide here, which are called the east, central and west groups.

According to studies carried out, researchers have concluded that Kabah existed prior to Uxmal, and it is very possible that demographic growth caused the inhabitants to move and settle in nearby areas. Today, we can see small ruins at places like Nohpat (between Kabah and Uxmal), Mul-Chic (near Santa Elena), Laltzuc (2 kms from Mul-Chic), Mesa Tunich and Postanil (along the highway to Campeche), Kancab (near the San Simón Hacienda), Sacpacal and Tzekelná, Sabacché (near the Hacienda of the same name), Tabi (near the Tabi Hacienda), and finally, Uxmal.

THE EAST GROUP

The most important part of Kabah is the east group, located across the paved highway. The buildings and reliefs can be better appreciated there because the buildings are better preserved.

On this side are two groups of buildings very close to each other. The first building sits on a high, wide terrace, and its exterior wall consists of three narrow, superimposed platforms; in the middle of the east side, a steep stairway gives access to the terrace. In the center of this terrace is a cistern which has been repaired and is still in use. In front of it, on the north side, is a small rectangular platform, about 70 cms high, that had been covered with intricate and enigmatic hieroglyphs; only a portion of these can be seen, as the remaining stones with their respective carv-

Platform with hieroglyphic carvings at Kabah. Photo by the author.

ings are being protected against deterioration. These hiero-. glyphs have not been placed back in the platform, as the correct order is unknown. It is assumed that this platform was used for ceremonies.

South of this terrace is a mound that used to be super-imposed platforms, on top of which a building had been built. Only portions of its foundation still exist, because on falling down, the stones and mortar rolled away giving it the shape it now has. A portion of the stairway is also still visible.

THE CODZ-POOP OR PALACE OF MASKS -- East of this terrace, on a low platform with seven steps, the visitor can admire one of the most beautiful buildings erected in the Maya area, particularly with respect to the components of its extensive façade. The pieces were cut, shaped and smoothed with such precision and finesse that they do not seem to have been fashioned with rudimentary and primitive stone tools.

Any one who carefully looks at the magnificence of this extraordinary façade has to agree that this is one of the more notable architectural marvels of the ancient Mayas. Its four sides, which are quite long, were totally covered by masks of the so-called rain god, as well as other intricate reliefs, all of which were probably painted in bright colors; in the mouths of some of these masks it is still possible to see vestiges of orange paint.

It seems that very few writers have paid attention to the quality of this magnificent structure, because when they describe it, they fail to mention how outstanding it really is.

On restoring the front façade, two heads were found among the rubble; they were very similar in appearance to the figure named the "King of Kabáh". One was taken to the Museum of Anthropology in Mexico City, the other to the Museum of Anthropology in Mérida, where it remains on display. The faces have haughty expressions, moustaches, and a hole through the cartilage of the nose, probably for insertion of a nose ornament, which was a common practice among the high-ranking Maya.

An oddity that we have noticed in the relief carvings of figures at Kabáh, is a tattoo that circles the eye (generally the left), continues down the cheek and ends in the middle of the chin below the lower lip, as in the case of the King of Kabáh, shown here.

This building is rectangular, approximately 46 meters long and 25 meters wide. It has five double chambers in front, each with its respective door. Most probably, the rear portion was the same, although it, as well as the north and south sides, are totally in ruins.

Partial - restoration was started along the front of the building, but the work was stopped some years ago. A large number of pieces were left in front of the building in their proper order, but unfortunately, some disappear almost every day, while others are broken by ignorant and irres-

74

This was the condition of the Codz-Poop Palace prior to restoration. Ilustration No. 56 a). Page 328 from the book La Civilización Maya by Sylvanus G. Morley.

The Codz-Poop after partial restoration. Photo by the author.

ponsible visitors, mostly pseudo students, who have thrown them around in all directions. The maliciousness of these people is such that they once tore off all the stones forming one of the rain gods located in the last chamber on the right hand side. Fortunately this was repaired, but the other carved stones belonging to this building, all of them irreplaceable national treasures, go on disappearing and being smashed.

This magnificent façade consists mainly of hundreds of rain god masks, put together by many sculpted segments

75

The least destroyed portion of the Codz-Poop. Photo by the author.

embedded in the wall and forming a mosaic. The eyes are single stones about 15 cms long, cut ready to be set in the wall. The square ears are fashioned in two segments with a hole in the middle; phallic symbols were probably inserted there, as in the mask located in the upper part of the more restored section. In these masks, one can make out the eyebrows, eyelashes, mouths and teeth, foreheads, etc.

The first row of masks is at ground level; above these, forming a cornice that runs the length of the building, are cut stones that resemble bits of ribbon with stone circles over these, and immediately above, two stylized serpents intertwine. Over this cornice, the Mayas added three tiers of masks; over the last row, they added a beautiful cornice consisting of stones carved to look like folds, and on top, equidistantly placed rosettes. Some dentated stones were placed in a zigzag manner above these, with isosceles triangles filling the spaces in between; then two serpents are again intertwined. Above these serpents are three more tiers of masks; it is quite possible that the façade originally had another cornice similar to the middle one. Although the masks are very similar, there are some slight differences. Something that very few people have noted, is that the masks at ground level, each has two ears, except for the last three on the right, which, like the rest, have only one ear between each pair.

The year the World's Fair was being held in New York, a renowned artist from India came to visit the more important archeological sites in Yucatán. He had been commissioned to decorate his country's stand at the World's Fair, and I was fortunate enough to accompany him and be his tour guide.

At Kabáh, we saw some workmen digging among the rubble of this building, under the direction of an archeologist who happened to not be there at the time, and while we watched, they uncovered some beautifully carved door jambs. One of them depicted a nobleman in a menacing stance facing a plebian begging for mercy. On seeing this, the man from India quickly made a drawing of it which he took back with him as a souvenir.

Subsequently, I found out that these door jambs had been reburied, possibly to be used at a later date, when that section was scheduled for restoration, or to protect them against erosion or removal.

This structure has two names: the Palace of Masks of the Rain God, and the Codz-Poop, "codz" meaning rolled up and "poop" sleeping mat or bed roll. Maybe the Mayas of the Decadent Period thought the wide nose of a rain god found inside the central chamber, in front of the door to the second interior chamber was a rolled up sleeping mat.

The photographs here reproduced show this building before and after its restoration; as well as various carving details.

Drawing by Mario Esquiliano of the King of Kabah.

Another view of the Codz-Poop. Photo by the author.

THE PALACE OR SECOND HOUSE -- The second group of buildings is located on a natural rise that is actually lower than the Codz-Poop.

This group forms a rectangular patio, bordered by a two-story building on the east side. The first or ground floor is quite destroyed, with only the central chamber still standing. In front, it has a half arch which was the support for the staircase that went up to the second floor, in other words, the roof of the first floor was part of the terrace of the second floor.

The simplicity of the façade's decoration does not even compare to that of the Codz-Poop, and it is almost certain that this structure predated the former.

From the top of the doors and side walls, the roof of the second floor slants backwards or inwards instead of outwards as in the other buildings, perhaps this was to give the appearance of the straw-thatched huts from which the Maya originated. The architectural style is Puuc, and consists of small columns embedded between the tops of the doors and the upper cornice. There are three small columns followed by a smooth section of wall; this pattern is repeated along the whole length of the building. The upper cornice consists of two fillets separated by more short cylindrical columns, also called drums, and ends with a sash or band that juts outwards; its ornamentation is completed with a showy crest, similar to the one on the Codz-Poop.

If it is true that both the crests and the false façades were used from the 16th to the 18th Century, then the building can be dated to that era.

The visitor can see that two of the front doors on the second floor (one on the right, the other on the left) are wider and have a cylindrical column in the center. This is because the Mayas had not yet discovered that heavy wood could withstand the weight of wider spans better than stone and mortar; upon discovering this, the system was changed, as can be seen at Uxmal, where wood lintels predominated. However, during restoration, the wood was replaced by concrete because the ends of a number of wooden lintels had already been eaten away. This is another reason for saying that Uxmal postdated Kabáh.

SOUTH BUILDING OR TEOCALI -- The south side of this quadrangle is also bordered by a two-story building, with chambers all around it on both the first and second floors, although very few of them are still standing.

To reach the second floor, its builders added stairways on the north and west sides, of which only the foundations exist in the shape of ramps supported by half arches.

Apparently it was Stephens who named the second floor of this building Teocali (a Nahua word meaning house of god), and the east building the Second House and the Codz-Poop the First House.

The visitor will note that the north and west sides of this quadrangle show vestiges of one-story buildings, and that access to this patio was from the west, although it had exits at the four corners.

In the center of this patio there is a cave which seems to have been a cistern, the top of which has fallen in.

On one side of this quadrangle (to the north) are some large stair-stepped platforms. Under one of these, small

1841 drawing by Catherwood of the Palace or Second House Kabah.

The Palace of Kabah today. Photo courtesy of Macario Quiñones.

chambers were found that had angular vaulted roofs and a rectangular entrance only just large enough for a person to crawl through. It is believed that these small chambers were tombs, but it is not known if the discoverers of the first one, which is now empty, found human bones or funerary containers. It is hoped that all these will. be

Catherwood's depiction of the arch at Kabah.

Condition of the same arch prior to restoration. Plate No. 56 of Dr. Sylvanus G. Morley's book "The Maya Civilization".

81

The arch at Kabah today. Photo courtesy of Macario Quiñones.

further explored so that their contents may become known.

Approximately 250 meters east of this quadrangle, is a building similar to the House of the Turtles at Uxmal, which was braced some years ago as it had deteriorated considerably. About 15 meters in front of this building, there used to be a terrace which was probably used to collect rain water to be stored in an enormous cistern with two inlets. This structure was given the name of the Third House.

THE CENTRAL GROUP

The majority of the buildings in this small group have deteriorated so, it is impossible to imagine what they may have looked like in their heyday.

Towards the west, across the paved highway, is a mound about 30 meters long which appears to be the base of a platform on which a building had been set.

Towards the north, is an enormous pyramid which appears elliptical and of almost the same height as the one at

Uxmal. Along its front, one can see only vestiges of a broad stairway, and on top are the foundations of three chambers and some of their door jambs. The largest door jambs are almost 1.50 meters high and weigh approximately half a ton. It is not known how these people transported such great weights to these heights, although it may have been by means of long ramps and wooden rollers. The ramps would have been removed when the building was completed.

In front of this high pyramid, are ruins of a long, low platform.

Farther south is a small quadrangle totally covered by vegetation with long mounds bordering it. Towards the northeast (after the platform just described), there is another mound of medium proportions with a terrace in front that is about two meters high, and which probably had stairs leading to it.

Behind this mound, a white road, called "sac beh" by the Mayas, runs in a southerly direction from an unadorned arch, about ten meters tall. This arch rests on a rectangular platform that is about one meter high on the south side and two meters high on the north side.

In front, a ramp provided access to this platform, while the rear portion had comfortable steps. At the base of the steps one can clearly see the start of the white road which is said to have joined Uxmal with Kabáh, passing through Nohpat. This road is seven meters wide on the northern side and ten meters on the opposite side.

When the stucco covering the inside of the arch began to fall away, red hand-prints appeared on the walls; there are similar hand-prints in other Maya buildings. Of course, there have been those who absurdly insist that those hand-prints were made by bloody hands. At Uxmal, in a partially fallen arch of the building located west of the Temple of the Magician, one can still see hand-prints in blue paint.

In our book entitled "An Overview of the Maya World", we talk about the network of roads that the Mayas had, and its respective characteristics; a map of these roads is also included.

THE WEST GROUP

Little can be said about this section because almost all the structures are quite deteriorated due to the effects of time and the thick vegetation that has overrun them for so many years.

Aside from restoring the arch, the only work done here has been a periodic clearing. Slightly more than 20 years ago, the I.N.A.H., under the leadership of the experienced archeologist Ponciano Salazar Ortegón, restored the stairway on the north side of the arch, and braced some of the buildings on the west side.

Access to this group is somewhat difficult, as there are

only a few gaps or openings in the vegetation, which some-times close all together; one must go with machete in hand to visit there.

We believe that very few people have noticed that this western area rests on top of a low hill which rises so gradually beyond the arch that it is hardly noticeable.

Condition of the left corner of the westermost building of the three that form the West Group at Kabah. Photo by the author.

The rear part of another building of the three that form the West Group. The chamber on the opposite side is in better condition. Photo by the author.

Restored portion of another building in the West Group. Photo by the author.

About 300 meters southwest of the arch, and through a gap in the vegetation, one reaches an esplanade that the Mayas converted into a terrace and on which they built three interesting structures, now rather deteriorated. The most important is on the west, the next on the north, and the least important on the south.

The west side building is the best preserved; in its center is a ramp which supported the stairway to the second floor. In the chamber beneath this ramp, one can see the well-preserved decoration of the cornice located over the top of the doors. The ornamentation consists of some short cylindrical columns or drums, beautifully sculpted, and above these are two stylized and intertwined serpents, similar to those of the Codz-Poop.

The second floor is smaller and was built over the center portion of the first floor. Some of the chambers on the south side of this first floor are still standing, as can be seen from the photograph; the rest of the chambers no longer exist.

On the north side of this terrace is another row of double chambers, but only the one on the east end has its vaulted arch still intact; inside this chamber are various lintels of hard wood which belonged to some of the doors. The chambers on this side are also double, although the back room of the latter is destroyed, as can be seen from the photograph.

The south side of this terrace has a long chamber with its vaulted arch still in existence; however, the flat stones with relief carvings that formed the façade have all come loose.

Catherwood's drawing of the wood carving found inside the building known as the House of the red Hands.

These three buildings are not joined together, and each has its own exit to the outside.

If, while standing on the Codz-Poop, we look for the second floor of this group, we can see it above the tall vegetation, signifying that this group is, in fact, at a much higher elevation on a hill.

Returning along the same path, we find another narrow gap or opening leading northwards to a weed-covered esplanade. Here are three small buildings that were restored at the time the bracing work was done on the group described above. We include the photograph of one of these buildings which has a wide entrance with a cylindrical column in the center, and a narrow door on the extreme right. In this section there are also various unexplored mounds.

Hacking through the dense vegetation in a north by northwesterly direction, one reaches a large mound over 100 meters long resting on an artificial platform; at one end is another two-story structure. Its center, front, and rear chambers are quite well preserved, possibly because the ramp that supported the stairway to the second floor protected them. This building was named the House of the Red Hands because various, red-painted hands are imprinted on the vaulted arch.

According to Stephens, it was in this section that he found the priceless wood lintel which is reproduced here, and which he took back to his country with great difficulty. Unfortunately, not long afterwards, there was a fire in the Panorama building in New York, where the lintel was on display, and this ancient Maya work of art was lost forever.

It is also very sad to see that huge trees are still growing over and through these buildings, causing irreparable damage.

NEW HIGHWAY IN THE PUUC REGION
AND THE COLONIAL ROUTE

To make visits to the archeological sites of Sayil, Xlápak and Labná easier, a new highway has recently been built that although rather sinuous is well paved. It starts close to Kilometer 105 of the "Vía Larga" that runs from Mérida to Campeche.

This new highway passes by the above mentioned sites, continues through a vast agricultural region of mainly fruit orchards, and by a place called La Cooperativa. It then goes past the beautiful lighted caverns of Loltún, and through the progressive village of Oxkutzcab, also called "the Orchard of Yucatán", because thousands of tons of delicious fruits and vegetables are grown there. This is one of the richest townships in Yucatán, because it is self-supporting and its inhabitants so hard-working that they labor in their fields from sun up to sun down.

At Oxkutzcab, this highway connects with the road called the Colonial Route or Route of the Convents, which goes through such historical villages at Maní, Tipikal, Teabo, Chumayel, Mama, Tekit, the ruins of Mayapán, Telchaquillo, Tecoh, Acancéh (where there are two small pyramids of Teotihuacan influence), Kanasín, and ending in the city of Mérida.

To get to Sayil, take the above described new highway to Campeche, for about 5 kms, until you see the sign indicating the site's proximity; turn on to the side road to the right. About 200 meters farther in is the parking lot and the new office that sells admission tickets.

This region covers a number of square kilometers dotted with Maya ruins; the rolling hills (called "uitz" in Maya) and low mountains make a very pleasant drive. The soil is sometimes reddish, other times much darker and very fertile.

Like at other ceremonial centers in this area, there are no lakes, cenotes or natural sources of water, which is why a considerable number of cisterns have been located.

Unofficially, we heard that Professor Jerry Sabloff was in Sayil in 1983, together with other archeologists, to explore this site. They indicated that more than 600 cisterns had been found, and they assume that many more are still hidden somewhere in the jungle.

This research work is very valuable, because knowing the number of cisterns and their water storage capacity, it is possible to calculate the number of people that lived here during its time of glory.

Prior to the building of this highway, which covers the important tourist circuit described, visitors had to resort to jeeps and landrovers to get to the Puuc region. These tours were primarily managed out of the Hacienda Uxmal Hotel by my friends, the Arana family, headed by the popular Hector, together with his brother Omar, who was a great personal friend of mine, and whose amiable, honest, sincere and helpful nature endeared him to all who had the good fortune to know him. These men, together with my late friend Crecencio Castillo and the young tour guide Jorge Lara, served all of Mérida's travel agencies, as well as arranging some private tours.

Passengers were generally picked up in Uxmal or Kabáh. On leaving the Campeche highway, the road became a broken rut, sometimes strewn with rocks and other times so steep that front-wheel drive had to be used, but in spite of the low speed, the rough terrain was body-shattering.

During the rainy season, the wheels of the vehicles frequently got stuck in the mud, and the drivers worked hard at overcoming these and other obstacles, having to be not only expert drivers but excellent mechanics as well just to negotiate this road; it was also necessary to carry major spare parts and tools in case of breakdowns.

The round trip to Uxmal took seven hours, including an hour for lunch. The travel agencies used to bring box lunches, including fruit and dessert, and an ice box with soft drinks. Lunch would be eaten in the shade of large trees at benches and tables which no longer exist.

During the rainy season, one had to avoid hundreds of horseflies (huge, blood-sucking flies), whose sting has been compared to a cigarette burn. During the dry season, one had to carefully avoid any contact with leaves that were covered with "pinolillos", diminutive ticks that would congregate by the hundreds on a leaf; if brushed against, the ticks would jump off and spread on to the person's skin, causing great discomfort and having to be removed one by one.

Along this rutted road, such wildlife as deer, rabbits, peccaris (javalinas) and snakes could frequently be seen, and very occasionally a jaguar; also many different birds, sometimes even the wild turkey with its brilliantly colored iridescent plumage. The odd thing about this wildlife is that they had no fear of motorized vehicles in spite of the noise, or of riders on horseback, but they were terrified by people on foot.

The trip's setbacks and adventures were more than compensated by the admiration felt for these incredible Maya builders.

One travel agency came up with the idea of selling overnight trips to Labná where some of the better preserved Maya chambers were made habitable, and the tourists slept in hammocks with mosquito netting. The jeep's driver then became the cook, carrying all the ingredients for delicious stews, as well as soft drinks and wines.

Since the inauguration of the new highway, things have changed -- the trip from Kabáh to Labná now takes only 20 minutes and only 35 minutes from Uxmal. One of the added attractions of the old days was a visit to the Sabacché cattle ranch, where an artificial well provided an unusual phenomenon: in the early morning a soft breeze started blowing from the bottom of the well, which grew stronger as the morning progressed and by noon it was blowing so hard you could hear the wind howl, and if you tried to throw something light, like a hat, into the well, the wind would blow it high into the air. As the sun started going down the force of the wind would decline until it disappeared completely; then it would reverse itself and pull air into the well with the same force as before, until it too disappeared during the night.

In trying to find out what caused this, I asked the man in charge of the ranch, and he said that when the well was built, and before the water reached it, a narrow tunnel appeared through which air blew and pulled. He also said that there was another such well in the neighbor state of Campeche, but there the owner had partially converted the tunnel with pipes that led to his house; he had installed a device that allowed him to regulate the force of the cold air flowing through the pipes, and used the system to air condition his house.

Eric S. Thompson, the archaeologist, made a visit to this area around 1926, and wrote about this well's odd feature, but obviously he did not believe it, because he says that he threw a light object into the well and it fell all the way to the bottom. Perhaps he visited the well very early in the morning or late in the afternoon when the movement of air is at the neutral point.

This author has observed this phenomenon numerous times when guiding tourists between 12 noon and 2 p.m. What we don't know is if this occurs every day or only in certain seasons or on certain days.

DESCRIPTION OF SAYIL

Sayil was not the original name of this site, it was so named by the Mayas long after it had been abandoned. The name comes from "say" the leaf-cutter ants so common in Yucatán, and the suffix "il" which means place -- the place of the leaf-cutter ants. Until a few years ago, near the main building, there were huge mounds of earth deposited by these ants after excavating their tunnels. These ants cut the leaves of trees that they find appetizing and carry them back to their underground tunnels, marching in long lines like soldiers. It is almost certain that at some time one Maya asked another where he was going and the first said, "To the place where the leaf-cutter ants are." One should not forget that the Maya language has a preponderance of monosyllabic words.

The layout of the buildings at Sayil is very similar to the one at Kabáh, and is divided into three groups: the north, the central, and the south, all of which were joined by a white road. Parallel to this road are numerous small mounds, particularly in the south group, of buildings now in ruins and covered by vegetation.

The tour of this site starts behind the ticket office; and about 150 meters to the southeast rises the impressive three-story building known by the name of "The Palace", a photo of which is shown here.

If totally restored, this building would rival the Governor's Palace at Uxmal, in size, beauty and proportions. It is rectangular in shape, measuring 92 meters long and 41 meters wide, with 85 chambers distributed in the following manner: 44 on the first or ground floor, 34 on the second and seven on the third floor.

Relatively little restoration work has been done on this building. The rear portion and the east side are quite destroyed and little is known about the original appearance of these, but it is almost certain that they were the same as the western section, which is the one that was used to calculate the total number of chambers. The first or ground floor has all the features of the Classic Puuc architecture, while the second floor is a mixture of the Puuc and Chenes

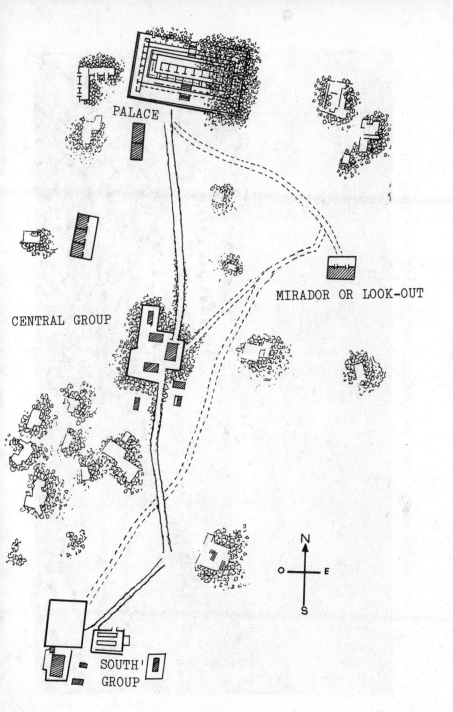

PALACE

MIRADOR OR LOOK-OUT

CENTRAL GROUP

N

O   E

S

SOUTH GROUP

Sketch of Sayil.

The Palace at Sayil. Photo courtesy of José López Nájera.

Hypotetical restoration of the Palace at Sayil by Tatiana Proskouria-koff; Photo No. 14 from her "Album of Maya Architecture".

styles. The third floor, which is assumed to be of a later date, has a very simple façade; over the top of the doors is a cornice consisting of three strips or bands. The two bottom ones are separated by short little drums.

If the inside were fully explored, we would definitely know if the third floor was built first over a raised pyramid

Section of the same Palace of Sayil. Photo by the author.

Detail of the same Palace. Photo courtesy of Javier Medina Riancho.

base, and the other floors added around it later, or if the reverse was done.

One of the major decorative elements of this region are the cylindrical columns embedded in the walls with narrow strips or bands in the center and sometimes on the ends as well.

On the left-hand corner of the second floor, the most beautiful part, there is a rain god similar to those frequently found; after it, towards the right, are 12 embedded cylindrical columns, and after these, a strange mask consisting of two separate squares which are assumed to be the eyes, and below them a stylized nose. Between the eyes, one can see a human figure, up side down, with legs spread wide. Similar up side down figures are found at Tulum (on the Caribbean coast of the state of Quintana Roo) an they have received the name of "Descending God".

On either side of this mask are open-mouthed lizards. Where the lizards' ears might be, are beautifully worked rosettes with many petals, and at the end of their tails is a ball with two feathers. Some writers and archeologists have mistaken these lizards for serpents. In the center of the left side, is a mask very different from the others, because its teeth are shown by six down-curving hooks. After that mask, the decorations and details described on the left side are repeated. Along the top of the building runs a cornice with two strips or bands divided by small drums (short stone cylinders) embedded in the wall.

A broad stairway with wide, raised sides was built to get to the top. This stairway was restored up to the level of the second floor. The existence of another narrow stairway was found on the opposite side.

About 60 meters northeast of this Palace, is a recently restored cistern that provides water for the employees that guard and clean this site. Fortunately, a new building has been built with rest rooms and a well for drinking water, it is hoped that it will soon be open for use.

When Eric S. Thompson visited the Palace, he jokingly compared it to an apartment house, but it probably housed offices used in the administration of this region. It is quite possible, however, that one or more of these floors were used as residences for the most important administrators.

The visitor will note that, like at Kabáh, the chambers that have wide entrances were built with cylindrical columns in the center; this tells us that the Mayas of that period had not yet discovered the fact that hard wood lintels could withstand the weight of wide spans better than the limestone lintels.

About 400 meters in the direction of the above described cistern, and across the highway, is a house built on top of a natural hill. Only two chambers still exist and they were restored not long ago. A stairway on the south side provided access, but only vestiges are still visible.

The present-day Mayas call this building "Bolomppel

Pol" (bolomppel means nine and pol means head), the Nine Heads. All the faces are different, but only five heads are still set in the wall.

About five meters west of the Palace, are some low mounds laid out in an L or right angle; the chambers are in ruins but parts of their vaulted arches can still be seen.

Another group of chambers in front of the Palace is in about the same condition; and at about 60 meters to the right, is another destroyed building.

The road that leads to the other groups starts in front of the Palace, but it is totally overgrown with vegetation and impassable. It is easier to follow the path going southeast to arrive at another building which has the ridiculous name of "Mirador" (lookout point); comments on this will be made under the description of Labná, where there is a similar building.

Before reaching the Mirador, one can take a path leading off to the right to arrive at the central group, which consists of some very deteriorated buildings. One structure stands out, in which can still be seen six small chambers with only three in fair condition. In the second chamber, the door jamb has various finely-carved hieroglyphs.

The white road goes from this group of buildings to the south group, where there appears to have been a small ball court. Farther west is a two-story building which appears to have been important. Its façade faces west and seven doors of different widths are visible. Its decoration consists of embedded, cylindrical columns, with a strip or band along the middle.

Nothing can be said about the second floor because it is totally in ruins.

Not far to the west of this building is a group of quite eroded stellae. Aside from the described structures, there are a number of small mounds as yet unexplored.

On the southwest side of the Mirador is an unusual cistern. Some 20 years ago, this author saw on its stucco walls drawings of frogs and fish, and a naked female figure seen from the back as if trying to scale the wall of the cistern and climb out. A guard here told me that this represented a woman giving birth. This discovery also caused some painful wasp stings, as a number of these winged insects lived in the partially ruined cistern.

About 200 meters away, along a path running in the same direction, the stone statue of a man about 2 meters tall was found lying on the ground. Due to the carelessness of the local peasants who usually burn the brush prior to planting their corn fields, this statue was found split in two sections. This male figure used to stand upright with his knees slightly spread, and rather surprisingly, particularly to visitors, the figure's male sex organ is so exaggerated that it reaches beyond his knees. To protect the statue, it has been set on a supporting pedestal and has been given a palm-thatch roof.

It is not known if the figure so represented was part of a legend, or if it was the work of a long ago Maya sculptor with an odd sense of humor.

DESCRIPTION OF XLAPAK

Seven kilometers from Sayil, is another short road leading off to the right that goes to Xlápak.

This name is composed of "Xlá" a derogatory way of saying old, and "pak" meaning wall, thus the old wall. In the Maya language, when an X precedes the word old (láb), its intent becomes derogatory.

As in the case of Sayil and other abandoned archeological sites, the original names are unknown, and after the downfall of their culture, the Mayas who visited had to call the place something; in this case they must have said they were going to visit the place of the old wall. This expression was probably used because the few buildings remaining there were so destroyed that they seemed to be just old walls.

There is very little to see here. The most important building was partially restored by the I.N.A.H. relatively recently, under the direction of César Sáenz, whom we have already mentioned.

This building is 21 meters long by 16 meters wide and has a total of nine chambers: three face east; one faces north and another south; and on the west side, there are two chambers in the center (one in front, one in the back), and one on either side. The two on the north end have

The most important building at Xlápak. Photo courtesy of Macario Quiñones.

fallen into ruin.

One thing we wish to point out is that the chambers along the west side are wider than the others, and although relatively low, the false arch was successfully used without the roofs caving in. It can be seen that the Mayas were very close to conceptualizing the real arch, however, they never did use it.

The ornamentation on this side, over the central doorway, consists of two superimposed masks which are similar to each other, but different from other masks. The lower one has a very wide mouth with 11 triangular teeth and eyes very close together and quite out of proportion to the mouth; the noses are shaped like hooks going in opposite directions from the masks on the corners. This is another example that these masks do not represent just one deity.

In front of this façade, is a cistern still in use, which provides water to the employees that guard and clean this site.

The façade on the west side is decorated with nine similar masks, three at each corner and another three over the central doorway; between each group of three, frets were added, and to complete the ornamentation, Vs were formed with five square stones, to which five small columns were added.

Both the central and the upper cornices, which wrap around all four sides of the building, consist of two strips or bands separated by short cylindrical columns or drums.

On the opposite side and very close to the cistern, is a mound about eight meters long that used to be chambers; although totally in ruins, a small portion of the Chenes style façade is visible.

About 300 meters northwest of this structure, are some chambers that were braced when the main building was restored. Some less important mounds have also been located in the surrounding areas.

DESCRIPTION OF LABNA

Five kilometers from Xlápak, a road leading to Labná branches off. There, like at Sayil, a new office has been built, with restrooms and a well for drinking water.

This site was named by the Mayas when its buildings were already practically in ruins. Its name comes from "lab" meaning old, and "nah" meaning house, and even though the name is written without the final "h" (Labná instead of Labnáh) it means old house. As already mentioned, after the Maya downfall, people visiting there would say they were going to the place of the old house, and the name stuck.

The importance of this place is due to the magnificent structure known today as The Palace, and its impressive arch, beautifully designed and decorated with extraordinary reliefs on both sides, as can be seen from the photograph.

This site has not been sufficiently explored, but it gives

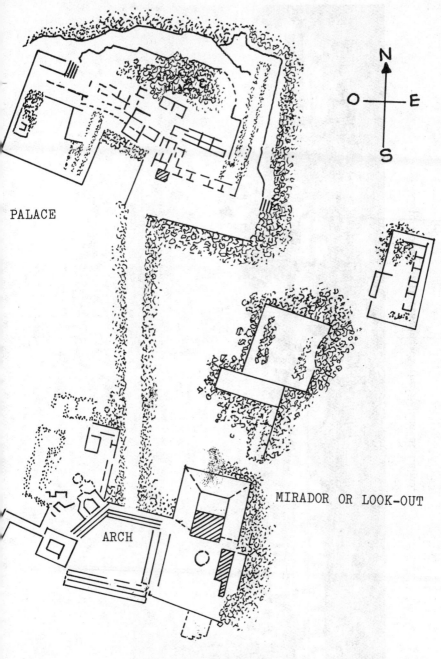

PALACE

N
O · E
S

MIRADOR OR LOOK-OUT

ARCH

Sketch of Labná.

Caterwood's 1841 drawing of the Palace at Labná.

Aereal view of Labná. In the foreground, the so-called Mirador; in the rear, The Palace. Photo by José López Nájera.

the impression of not being very large, in spite of this, however, it seems odd that a complex of these dimensions and category should have been built at this site.

As a result of this author's personal observations of the Palace building, he has come to the conclusion that it was built in seven different stages. It was not planned all at once; however, its builders tried not to disrupt the total esthetics with each addition, and in the end, they achieved a well-balanced harmony of the finished complex.

If we look at this complex cursorily, we get the impression that it is one long structure of two separate floors.

The section that runs right of center, rests on a platform that is about 2.5 meters high, and at one end, evidence of 10 chambers was found; these extend backwards in a straight line, towards the north.

The five chambers which jut forwards on the left (in front) are independent and have very simple ornamentation; thus, we believe they were built at an earlier time. Chamber number five, the foremost one, is totally in ruins.

Most probably, the order in which this Palace complex was built is the following:

a) The first stage would have been the three chambers, in good condition, that are on the left towards the front; their façades are Puuc style. Over each door are very strange masks; one sits over the other so closely that the forehead of the lower one becomes the teeth of the upper one.

b) The second stage would have been the following five chambers on the right. Of these five, the first has no

Central part of the Palace at Labná. Photo by the author.

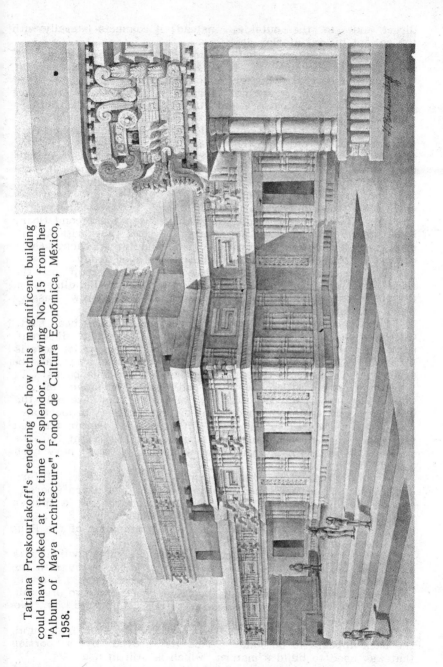

Tatiana Proskouriakoff's rendering of how this magnificent building could have looked at its time of splendor. Drawing No. 15 from her "Album of Maya Architecture", Fondo de Cultura Económica, México, 1958.

direct exit to the outside, instead, it connects laterally with the second by an interior door.

The visitor will note that these chambers were added at a later date because of three reasons: the first is that the five chambers are at a higher level than the first ones; second, because they are not aligned with the others (they are placed slightly forwards); and third, because its architectural style is closer to the Chenes.

c) The next addition would have been the chamber that was added in front of the five above and which is now almost non-existent; only a part of its lateral walls and half its vaulted arch remain. One can clearly see that it was subsequently added, because the Chenes style decoration that was previously on the outside, as it is now, can be seen at the rear of the chamber.

d) The next addition would have been the second floor, built along the back. According to some authorities, it consisted of four chambers in front and two in back. Only one section of wall and vaulted arch can be seen today.

e) The next stage would have been the group on the right at first-floor level. This was a separate building from the one above, as it was separated by a narrow passage which was later roofed with an angular arch.

This structure juts forwards, as has already been said. On the west façade, over the door, it has a rather different mask; its mouth has teeth that project forwards; its nose is broad with hieroglyphs on the concave curve, as can be seen in the various masks pictured on previous pages. To the left of this mask, an idol had been embedded in the wall. Its top part is missing, and one can see only the hips, legs and feet with boots on. From these proportions, if this represented a person of that period, we can tell that the Mayas were rather short and stocky. To the right of the mask is another hole where a similar idol must have been embedded.

At the corner of this building, is another mask, different again; from its open mouth, the jaws of a lizard emerge, and on the lizard's palate is a relief carving of a human face; the mask's nose is a concave upward curve.

The façade of the first floor is a combination of the Puuc and Chenes styles.

f) Most probably, the second floor of this section was added at a later date, so as to provide harmony with the previous building. It consisted of six chambers, four in front and two in back. Of the front chambers, two are still in good condition; its wide doorways are supported by two columns each.

The terrace in front is the roof of the first floor, and the back appears to be solid. This is proved by a portion that was used to build a cistern, which is still in use.

g) Lastly, the row of chambers on the far right (east side) would have been built. These are now totally in ruins.

If we compare this complex's present condition with the drawing made by Catherwood in 1841, we can see that it has deteriorated considerably during those intervening years.

EAST BUILDING -- About 80 meters east of the Palace, is a group of chambers that jointly form an L or right angle. The long side of the L is 30 meters long and consists of five chambers; the short side has only two chambers, of which the last is totally destroyed.

Its decoration is simple, consisting of a series of short cylindrical columns or drums bordered by two fillets along its middle and upper cornices. Between these two cornices, a series of short columns are embedded, covering the whole façade. This structure sits on a low platform that had narrow stairs at the front.

SOUTH GROUP

One hundred and thirty meters south of the Palace, is a group of buildings connected by an easily distinguished path. This group consists of a small pyramid to the left on which rests a structure that used to have four chambers, one at each end and a double one in the center; only the one on the west side is in good condition, the others have been reduced to rubble.

Some researchers call this structure the Great Pyramid, others call it the Mirador (Lookout Point). Both these names are inadequate -- this pyramid is in no way very large, nor was it ever a lookout point. Those who so named it must have mistaken its tall false façade for a lookout point because of the holes in it. When we described the west side of the so-called Cemetery Group at Uxmal, we explained the purpose of the false façades and crests (or ornamental superstructures) of the Maya buildings, and the reason for having the holes. In addition, no one has ever found a platform behind these architectural structures that could have indicated a place on which to stand and look out from.

In front of the platform on which this building rests, is a ramp which supported the stairway, and on one side, the front wall of a small chamber with its door and part of its vaulted arch, is clearly visible.

In front, is a small patio bordered on two sides by two small platforms, now in ruins. Towards the west is another small patio bordered on the east by one of these platforms; there is another one to the south and one more towards the north which connects with the path that comes from the Palace. To the west is the rear façade of the magnificent arch. To go through the arch, one climbs three comfortable steps.

The middle cornice on this side consists of dentated stones with triangles in between, like the cornice of the Codz-Poop at Kabáh. Above this are two frets that are joined by square stones stair-stepped to form a V, like the façade of the main building at Xlápak. Then comes another cornice, the bands or fillets of which enclose a series of carvings that look rather like a T. The ornamentation is completed by a low crest, as can be seen in the accompanying photograph.

Going through the arch, one arrives at another small patio, also rectangular, formed by the arch and various semi-destroyed chambers which are laid out northwards. The intact portion of the façade has some pretty geometric designs.

The rear or exterior facade of the arch at Labná. Photo courtesy of Gonzalo Cáceres and Porfirio Ocampo Camarena.

Te front or iterior facade of the Arch at Labná. Photo courtesy of Macario Quiñones.

Tatiana Proskouriakoff's rendering of the hypothetical restoration of this arch. Drawing No. 16 of her "Album of Maya architecture".

The chambers that used to be on the south, west and north sides have totally fallen into ruin.

The principal façade of the arch is here. On each side is a trapezoidal door, each leading into a small chamber, and over the doors is a beautiful cornice formed by dentated stones with triangles in between, as on the opposite side, and above each door is a straw-thatched hut carved in stone, the doors of which form hollow niches. It is assumed that there were idols sitting cross-legged in those niches, because inside are the stones that used to support them.

At the level of the thatched roofs, is the second cornice, and the third is over the top of the arch.

In Tatiana Proscouriakoff's hypothetical restoration, also shown, she depicts the three crests as they may have originally been.

The green and red painted spots still visible inside the niches indicate that the whole arch, and possibly all of Labná, was painted in bright colors.

Upon ending the visit to this site and on the way back to the parking lot, one can see in the shade of some trees, a very interesting group of sculpted stones. Some of these are flat and show figures of persons with intricate tufts of feathers, their knees slightly spread, and broad sashes around the waist, the ends of which fall down the front to their ankles. The scepters in their hands indicate people of high rank.

On another flat stone, one can see two back-to-back jaguars. In this group, there is also a phallic symbol,

Five heads with almost identical round faces and rather puffy cheks at Labna.

about 60 cms high and 25 cms in diameter. The most interesting object in this group, however, are five heads with almost identical round faces and rather puffy cheeks; they look almost oriental, and on the cap that adorns each head, are small protruberances which resemble horns. The features of these faces are totally different from the Maya.

The many different representations of human faces that have been found in the Maya territory, resembling people from other continents, disconcert and confuse the researchers more each day as they try to find out the real origin of the incredible and magnificent Mayas.

Finally, we would like to remind our readers that the archeological region known by the name of Puuc, is really rather extensive, and in this work we have described only the most important places that can be visited in a one day tour and still provide a pretty good idea of all that it involves. It is hoped that the personal efforts of this author -- who, as a tourist guide has dedicated the last 20 years to the detailed study of the Maya Culture -- have been to your liking and edification.

THE AUTHOR

BIBLIOGRAPHY

1) Barrera Vásquez, Alfredo, y Silvia Rendón. El libro de los Libros de Chilám Balám. Fondo de Cultura Económica, México, D.F. 1965.

2) Canto López, Antonio. Apuntaciones sobre Mesoamérica, Mérida, Yucatán, México. 1973.

3) Cordemex. Diccionario Maya Español y Español Maya. Ediciones Cordemex. 1980.

4) Civeira, Fabuada y Domingo Martínez Paredez. Yucatán visto por Fray Alonso Ponce (1588-1589) y Vocabulario de Palabras Mayas que figuran en la Obra de Fray Alonso Ponce. Ediciones de la Universidad de Yucatán. Mérida. 1977.

5) De Landa, Diego. Relación de las Cosas en Yucatán. Editorial Purrúa S.A., México D.F. 1962.

6) Instituto Nacional de Antropología e Historia de México. Uxmal, Official Guide. Talleres Edimex S.R.L., México D.F. 1959.

7) Liga de Acción Social. Códice Pérez. Dr. Solís Alcalá, traductor. Ediciones de la Liga de Acción Social, Mérida, Yucatán, México. 1949.

8) Morley, Sylvanus Griswold. La Civilización Maya. Fondo de Cultura Económica, México D.F. 1975.

9) Molina Solís, Juan Francisco. Historia del Descubrimiento y Conquista de Yucatán. Ediciones Mensaje, México D.F. 1943.

10) Meex, Claudio (Dr. Eduardo Urzáiz Rodríguez). Reconstrucción de Hechos. Copia facsimilar por José Díaz Bolio y J. Guy Puerto, Mérida, Yucatán. 1982.

11) Proskouriakoff, Tatiana. Album de Arquitectura Maya. Fondo de Cultura Económica. Traducción de Victor O. Moya. México D.F. 1969.

12) Roy, Ralph L. The Book of Chilam Balam. New Edition. University of Oklahoma Press, Norman, Okla. 1967.

13) Solís Alcalá, Ermilo. Diccionario Español Maya. Editorial Yikal Maya Than, Mérida, Yucatán. 1949.

14) Sáenz, César. Boletín No.36 del Instituto Nacional de

Antropología e Historia (I.N.A.H) de México. 1969.

15) Sansores Cirerol, Manuel. El Arte Pictórico de los Antiguos Mayas. Talleres Gráficos del Sudeste S.A., Mérida, Yucatán. 1955.

16) Sansores Cirerol, Manuel. Guía de Uxhmal. Segunda Edición. Talleres Gráficos del Sudeste S.A., Mérida, Yucatán. 1956.

17) Stephens, John L. Incidents of Travel in Yucatán. Two Volumes. Dover Publications Inc., New York, N.Y. 1963.

18) Thompson, J. Eric S. The Rise and Fall of the Maya Civilization. University of Oklahoma Press, Norman, Okla. 1966.

19) Thompson, J. Eric S. Arqueología Maya. Editorial Diana S.A., México D.F. 1978.